The Power
of
His Resurrection

By
T. Austin-Sparks

The Power of His Resurrection
All *new* material in this edition
copyrighted by SeedSowers Publishing House
Printed in the United States of America
All rights reserved

Published by The SeedSowers
          P.O. Box 3317
          Jacksonville, FL 32206
          1-800-228-2665

Library of Congress Cataloging - in - Publication Data

Sparks, T. Austin
          The Power of His Resurrection / T. Austin-Sparks
          ISBN 0-940232-83-9
          1. Spiritual Life   1. Title

Times New Roman 12pt

The Power
of
His Resurrection

Preface

T. Austin-Sparks is one of the great figures of the twentieth century who ministered outside of the organized church. For over forty years he held forth at Honor Oak in London, England. The conferences he spoke at, both in Europe and America, have had a profound influence on our time.

Brother Sparks published over one hundred books and pamphlets. The majority of them have ceased to be available to the Christian family. This has been a great loss, as the content of his message has placed him in the category of only a few men of the last one hundred years.

T. Austin-Sparks and Watchman Nee, more than any other men, have influenced the lives of believers who are outside traditional churches. We have felt very strongly that all of brother Sparks' books and pamphlets should be brought back into print if at all possible.

Read T. Austin-Sparks. It is our hope that in republishing these works, his ministry will take wings again, and the influence of his word will spread across the English-speaking world. Hopefully this will give his message a greater influence than ever before.

We send this book forth with a prayer that what he ministered will become realities in the 21st century.

The SeedSowers

.

Contents

CHAPTER I. A SURVEY 5
The Link Between Elisha and Elijah—The Waters of Jericho—The Three Kings in League—The Widow's Oil—The Woman's Son—The Poisoned Pottage—Naaman, the Syrian Leper—The Loose Axe-head—The Feeding of the Multitude —The Unseen Horseman—The Arrows—Elisha's Death— Elisha's Preparation in His Natural Vocation—Everything of Spirit—The Test of Faith and Perseverance—Learning the Secret of Power From on High—Having His Beginnings in Jordan.

CHAPTER II. THE WATERS OF JERICHO 19
I. The Inclusive Representation of Calvary's Victory Over the Power of Satan Working Through the Flesh. Jericho (a) Something Too Strong for Man. (b) Fullness as Represented by "Seven." (c) Achan. II. The Omnipotence of Faith in the Power of the Cross. III. The Curse Resting Upon All the Satan-Energized Works of Achan. (a) Death. (b) Vanity— Elisha's Roots Are in Jordan—Elisha's Authority Is in Anointing—Elisha's Vessel Is a New Cruse—Elisha's Means Is Salt.

CHAPTER III. ELISHA AND THE SONS OF THE PROPHETS ... 33
The Sons of the Prophets—Who and What They Were—That Which Elisha Represents.

CHAPTER IV. THE NATURE OF THE LIFE AND TESTIMONY OF THE LORD'S PEOPLE 50
I. The Valley Filled With Water—Resurrection Life in the Midst of Pressure From a Hostile World Outside—The Widow's Oil. (a) The State of the Church. Unable To Meet Obligations. (b) The Power of the World Over "the Church." (c) A Little Oil—The Shunammite's Son—The Supreme Need. Fullness of Resurrection Life.

CHAPTER V. THE HEALING OF NAAMAN 65
    The Natural Man—A New Attitude Towards the Instrument
    Used for His Spiritual Good—Naaman Worshiped Jehovah—
    His Resources at the Lord's Disposal.

CHAPTER VI. THE THRONE IN HEAVEN 77
    I. The Opening of the Eyes of Elisha's Servant. II. Blindness
    Brought to the Syrian Host—The Fact of Union With the
    Lord—The Nature, Basis and Place of This Union—The
    Issue of Union Is Government—The Law of Union Is Faith.

CHAPTER VII. CLOSING SCENES 89
    I. The Arrow of the Lord's Deliverance. II. The Smiting on
    the Ground With the Arrows. III. The Revival of a Dead
    Body by Contact With Elisha's Bones.

Elijah types of Jesus Christ

The Power of
His Resurrection

CHAPTER ONE

A Survey

The Link Between Elisha and Elijah

The second book of Kings has very largely to do with the life and ministry of Elisha, the prophet; and Elisha undoubtedly brings before us the Old Testament illustration and type of the Church living and working in the power of resurrection. We are familiar with the point at which the ministry of Elijah gives place to that of Elisha. When the Lord took up Elijah in a chariot of fire to heaven, Elisha's connection with that rapture, that ascension, was a matter of his being on the spot and seeing his master taken up, and of having fulfilled in himself the request that he should receive a double portion of the spirit of Elijah.

Elijah thus very clearly becomes a type of the Lord Jesus ascending, and the Holy Spirit as a double portion of His Spirit coming upon the Church, fulfilling His own words: ". . . Greater works than these shall he do; because I go unto the Father." In the case of the Lord Jesus the Church followed, proceeding in the fullness of the Spirit to work out the ministry of Christ on a larger scale than He in the days of His flesh had been able to accomplish. His own prayer in those days was that the baptism with which He had to be baptized might be accomplished, because He had come to scatter fire on the earth. That scattering could not be until the baptism of the Cross was a realized thing, and He longed therefore for His emancipation from the limitations of the flesh. When that baptism of passion was fulfilled, and He was translated to the glory, the fire was scattered in the earth, and His desire was fulfilled through His Church; His limitations were removed.

That has its foreshadowing in the ministries of Elijah and Elisha. So that which came in with Elisha is that which comes in with the Church—fullness by the Spirit in the power of resurrection. There we begin, with Elisha coming in on resurrection ground for the purpose of showing forth the fullness of the ascended Head. The fact that Elisha does speak of the power of resurrection, and the full meaning of life on that ground, is amply borne out by the outstanding incidents of his life. If you cast your eye over them you will see that it is, firstly, a matter of changing from death to life, and then, secondly, of changing from limitation to fullness.

We begin with

The Waters of Jericho,

cruse

the new cruse and the salt. By these means the waters were healed, and the fruit of the ground delivered from the bondage of death and corruption, and made living, abiding, and full. Then

The Three Kings in League

were in a most paralyzing situation for want of water, in danger of being delivered into the hands of Moab. There was the digging of the trenches in the valley by faith, and silently, without noise or demonstration, the torrents of water coming down; then the deliverance from captivity to the enemy, from the hand of the spoiler. It is the power of resurrection life in fullness.

The Widow's Oil

A calamity had overtaken her, leaving her in a predicament. There were the vessels, not a few. The fullness of life is typified in the poured forth oil, the limitation of which was not on the Divine side but on the human side. Then we have

The Woman's Son,

given, taken, raised from the dead. That speaks for itself as to the power of resurrection, and as to the fullness of life.

The Poisoned Pottage

The sons of the prophets found death in the pot, and by the casting in of the meal the death elements were destroyed—death turned to life, fullness, and satisfaction.

Next we have

Naaman the Syrian Leper,

his washing (if you like, his baptism) in Jordan; all of which speaks for itself to those who know anything of the meaning of Jordan—from death unto life, the fullness of the power of His resurrection.

The Loose Axe Head

We have the sons of the prophets again, building their place of instruction; the incident of the axe head coming off; falling into the water and sinking; the casting in of the branch of the tree, causing the iron to float. Once more is seen the miracle of life triumphant over death, and fullness of satisfaction. There follows

The Feeding of the Multitude

with a small amount of bread;

The Unseen Horsemen

in the day of peril and threatened death;

The Arrows,

which were the arrows of deliverance; and finally

Elisha's Death,

and a man brought to life by touching his bones.

So Elisha, from start to finish, is a most conspicuous type of the power of resurrection, and of what that means as fullness of life.

All these are aspects of the one comprehensive truth, and each has its own particular message to bring in connection with it. We are not going to touch any of them in particular until later. They have been reviewed simply for the purpose of getting our minds clear as to what Elisha really stands for, and of giving us a further point from which to move forward.

Elisha's Preparation in His Natural Vocation

That which will occupy us now is connected with the preliminary stage in Elisha's life, before he moved out into this full expression. There is always a preparatory stage, and a preparatory dealing with us on the part of the Lord.

The first time Elisha comes before our notice is very significant of what the Lord takes account of, when He puts His hand upon a man or a woman, to make such a vessel of His fuller Testimony. It is found in 1 Kings xix.19-21:

> So he departed thence, and found Elisha the son of Shaphat, who was plowing, with twelve yoke of oxen before him, and he with the twelfth: and Elijah passed over unto him, and cast his mantle upon him. And he left the oxen, and ran after Elijah, and said, Let me, I pray thee, kiss my father and my mother, and then I will follow thee. And he said unto him, Go back again; for what have I done to thee? And he returned from following him, and took the yoke of oxen, and slew them, and boiled their flesh with the instruments of the oxen, and gave unto the people, and they did eat. Then he arose, and went after Elijah, and ministered unto him.

Here you have some features of a life upon which the Lord looks, or has already looked, with a view to bringing that life into relationship with Himself and His Testimony in a way of fullness. The characteristics of Elisha here are such as the Lord looks for in His would-be servants.

What Elijah found was a man of whom, by reason of his thoroughness in what he did, a note was made in the Divine records, which goes down through the ages. He was ploughing with twelve yoke of oxen. He was putting all his resources into the work. In his ordinary course of life he was not having anything in reserve. Twelve yoke of oxen represent the doing of things thoroughly; doing what your hands find to do with all your might. Oxen are types of strength in service, and, although Elisha was but in his ordinary natural vocation, in that there were no half-hearted measures. He was doing it with a downrightness that is taken account of. It may seem to be a very simple thing, but the Lord puts His workers on a probation to watch for that very thing. We may be waiting for the time when we shall be able to serve the Lord with all our might and main, and in the waiting time we may be reserving ourselves just a little along other lines. That can be put in different ways, but you may take it as settled the Lord will never put you into a ministry of manifesting the power of His resurrection, of being of any special value to Him in His Testimony, if He has seen slothfulness in the ordinary walks of life, if He has observed any trace of half-heartedness in other directions. There is an infinite peril associated with waiting for what we call our life work. The waiting should be of a positive character, and during that time we should be in nothing less than a hundred per cent energy in what there is about us to do.

This is a word of warning, and a word that we are constrained to give. It is not the sort of thing we like to say, and yet it is a word which those of us who have had time to observe, to watch the preparation of many lives for the work of the Lord, feel to be a necessary word. We mark how that the time before the Lord can visit a life and say, "Now the hour has come for you to move out into that for which I have prepared you," is a time that is so often marked by a lack of whole-hearted abandonment to the ordinary natural vocation; that the things which we call "natural" are put in a place second to the spiritual, and regarded as of less importance, and as calling therefore for much less diligence.

We need not increase words, but it is a thing for us all to guard very carefully. The Lord is watching in the ordinary vocations of life, in the things which we may regard as by no means of any great spiritual value, to see if in those very things we are diligent. We must remember that His own words are: "He that is faithful in that which is least is faithful also in much." That is a law; and faithfulness in that which is least is qualification for increase.

On the other side, when the Lord sees a man (or a woman) who, like Elisha, is putting all his energy, all his resources into his ordinary vocation, and doing it with all his might, the Lord marks that man (or that woman), and the time will come when that life will be drawn into association with the Lord in something of peculiar value to Him.

You see this in the first phase, before any thought or suggestion had come to Elisha of prophetic ministry. It is not as if he were as one of the sons of the prophets preparing for his ministry. No suggestion whatever is made that he is to be a prophet. We do not know that he had any such idea. What we do know is that he was doing farm work, and that he was putting all his might into it, and the Lord took account of it. Before ever there was a thought of, what many people would call, spiritual work, this man was seen by God as one who would go a long way with Him. Of course Elisha was a godly man, not just a man of the world diligent in his business.

You may say: That is reckoning on the natural. Well, the Lord does take men into account as to their spirit, and although a man may be very often mistaken as to the method, and as to the way, the Lord looks on the heart. We are thinking of Paul himself. He was certainly very blind, and very mistaken in the way that he took, but he took it with all his might, and there was no

question that what he did was with every ounce of his being, and
we are not to say that the Lord did not take that into account.
The Lord takes account of diligence and devotion and whole-
heartedness, in whatever realm it is. When the Lord gets hold of
men and women of that kind, He may have deep and mighty
lessons to teach them, but He knows that He has a vessel that
will be suitable to Him, and that will go on with Him.

That is a simple word, almost in the nature of a homily, but
it is an important one, and we must never expect the Lord to say:
"Come up higher," until we have given ourselves to the very last
measure in the place where we are. We rejoice that there are men
and women like Elisha, who just put themselves into the menial
things, the ordinary things, the things which men would not call
specifically spiritual service, until the Lord says, "That is
enough." This is preparation; and remember the Lord is taking
account!

Everything of Spirit

The next thing in the case of Elisha follows closely upon
the intimation that he was called. Elijah threw his mantle over
him. Then it looked as though Elisha drew back; it looked as
though he might be numbered with certain in the New Testament
who said: "first suffer me to bid farewell to them that are at my
house"; "Lord, suffer me first to go and bury my father"; and
soon. But there is the fact that something deeper had been registered in Elisha, which did not allow him to do the thing he had
contemplated doing. We do not read of any farewells in the way
he suggested them to Elijah; but what we do read is that he went
and rid himself of all that was behind. He burned his bridges,
cleared up things straightway, distributed the proceeds, and went
after Elijah. Again, the marks of thoroughness!

Here is a man who is not saying: "Well, in case things go
wrong, and I do not get on very well in my new sphere of work,
I had better keep these oxen alive, so that I can come back to
this!" The thing had gone to his heart. He knew the hour had

struck; he knew God had touched him; deep down in his being there was something which had made him a prisoner, from which he found no release; so he simply cleared up everything, and went in the way of that inward call.

The point is mainly this, that it was not Elijah's call that did it. On the strength of Elijah's word alone Elisha could look back; that is, he could contemplate going to have a valedictory; but there was something deeper than Elijah's word. Something had come through from God into his inner being, which put away all that was merely sentimental or earthly, and made him do a thorough work of breaking, and going out for the Lord. It is important for us to hear something deeper than the voice of man when we move into the work of the Lord. We must have something more than the outward appeal. We can have many appeals, strong urges, in meetings arranged for that purpose, to appeal for workers. We can have the appeal from the outside. We can have the urge. We can even have people tell us that we ought to go, that God has really called us. But that is never enough. What we must know is that God has spoken more deeply than any kind of outward appeal. We must know that God has done something, and that because of this there is no question for us whatever of keeping in reserve the old relationships, the old associations, the old interests; that deeper challenge has settled everything, and the only thing we can do is to make a complete break, and go out with the Lord.

Again, this is very elementary, but it is very important. A great many go out on the strength of an appeal, or an urge of man, and that is always a very dangerous thing. It is equally dangerous for us to put our hands upon people, and to tell them what they ought to do, what God would have them do, what and where their call is. Let us seek to keep our hands off people altogether as to their life, and leave them with the Lord. Run a thousand miles from them rather than try in any way to shape their life course for them. If God does not speak, we shall only make havoc of lives in trying to influence them of ourselves. We must never be influenced by anything but the Word of the Lord in our heart. Someone may speak, and through that someone there may strike home like a shaft the word of the Lord, but we must have that extra element before there can be certainty. When we have that, we know it; God has spoken, and everything is changed.

It is interesting that we hear nothing more of Elisha from that day, until the day when Elijah finishes his ministry. It is fitting that it should be so. In 2 Kings ii. Elisha comes in in connection with the translation of his master, Elijah. There are three things in that chapter which are factors in this preliminary stage in the preparation of this vessel of the Testimony.

I. The Test of Faith and Perseverance

The first thing is Elisha's test of faith and perseverance after he had received the knowledge of a call. You notice and it is a familiar story how Elijah, on the one hand, seemed to be trying to shake off Elisha: "Tarry here . . ." "Tarry here . . ."; "Tarry here. . . ." To every such urge of Elijah, Elisha rejoined: "As the Lord liveth, and as thy soul liveth, I will not leave thee." On the other hand the sons of the prophets in every place they visited said: "Knowest thou that the Lord will take away thy master from thy head to day?" seeking to discourage, to deter him. There is no element of encouragement about this repetition. Elisha replies: "Yea, I know it; hold ye your peace." It makes no difference to me: I am going to follow on to the end: I am going to see this thing through. It may be the Lord's will to take him away, but I am going to be there when it happens. And so, whatever the meaning of Elijah's repeated effort to get him to stay may have been, he could not influence this man one bit, could not shake him off. Elisha was exercising faith, with a persistence and endurance which is the outstanding feature of this chapter.

In what connection is his faith being exercised, and in what connection is his persistence being tested? Well, Elijah has what he needs! It comes within that realm of some being discouraged, being able to be put off, and saying, while others go on, "These are hard sayings, who can hear them?" "From that time many of his disciples went back, and walked no more with him." They are discouraged more or less easily, and they go away. And the Lord turns to the twelve and says: "Will ye also go away?" Simon Peter answers: "Lord, to whom shall we go? thou hast the words of eternal life." The Master has what is needed, and there is no thought of going away, being put off, discouraged, but the thought is to go on with Him, because He has the essential elements of that life. Elisha knew that Elijah had what he needed for his life, for his ministry. So that when Elijah said: "Ask what I shall do for thee," Elisha replied: "Let a double portion of thy spirit be upon me." Elijah's rejoinder was: "Thou hast asked a hard thing: nevertheless, if thou see me when I am taken from thee, it shall be so unto thee. . . ." Elisha knew that Elijah had the essential, and was not to be put off, or easily discouraged. Although it seemed that Elijah was trying to get rid of him, the other man refused to be got rid of; he was clinging to him for life. He was, moreover, being tested as to his faith, and as to his perseverance.

It is a part of Elisha's preparation, and that of all true instruments of the Lord. They will go through experiences in which they are tested to the very last ounce of endurance, along the line of it seeming to be that even the Lord is trying to shake them off. That is a very crude way of putting it; but so often there is every opportunity, if you are ready to accept appearances alone, to be discouraged, to feel the Lord does not want you, that after all, although you may have had the sense of a call, the Lord is not going through with it. Rather it looks as though you are being put back, and put back again. Can you be discouraged? Can you be shaken off? Can your faith easily give way? If so, you are of little use for this calling. If you are going to be an instrument of the Testimony of the power of His resurrection, you are going to have a very great deal that you will come up against, that will put you out of the fight, if you can be put out. It is very necessary to be established before you start; in some measure that proves that you are not one to be easily put off, easily discouraged.

Elisha went through the test; on the one hand, his own master being the occasion of the testing, and on the other hand, those who were in a spiritual position, sons of the prophets—supposed to be the people who had spiritual knowledge—being anything but encouraging, rather being discouraging factors. Very often those who ought to be helpful by reason of their spiritual position—officially, at any rate—are anything but encouraging; they would put us back. All that we are left with is: The Lord has called me; I know that in my heart. The Lord has led me this way. The Lord has caused me to take this step that I have taken. I have burned my bridges; I have cut all my ties; I have stepped out on the Lord. Now, although I have done that, the Lord is testing me, seeming to give me very little confirmation and encouragement, and the Lord's representatives (officially) are by no means helpful: Nevertheless I stand to it, I am going on with God. A man or a woman who can go on like that is going to count for God. Elisha had nothing whatever to fall back upon save his inward knowledge of the Lord. He went through on that.

It is a very nice thing when we get encouragement from every direction in the way of our conceived call; when the Lord comes along and confirms it in all sorts of ways, and then everyone else, and everything else, says: "We are with you; we will stand by you; we are going to support and uphold you." We can get on all right that way. But if the Lord gives us no special conspicuous providences, sovereign acts; if He hides Himself, so that what we do see is rather discouragement from going on, even from the Lord's side (and one of the most difficult things is the hiding of the Lord, though He is there hiddenly doing things, and marvelously carrying through unto enlargement and enrichment, while allowing nothing that the flesh can take hold of), then it is a matter of faith going on with God, even when the Lord seems to be hiding Himself, and allowing much of discouragement to remain on our horizon. At such a time no one else can enter into it. Everybody else to whom we might look, and from whom we might expect something, is of no use to us at all.

All that they have to say is something that is melancholy: "Knowest thou that the Lord will take away thy master from thy head to day?" Elisha seems to be a little impatient with that. It might have been expressed in this way: You are a morbid crowd, and I would sooner you kept quiet if you have nothing better to say! They are not inspiring at all. And that is very often how we find the people to whom we look for encouragement. They see the difficulties, they see the dark side of things, they tell us of what we are running our heads into, of the calamities that will overtake us. The question is: Will you go on with God? Elisha went on! The statement is: "They two went on." There is something in that which leads to a large place, which means much for the Lord.

II. Learning the Secret of Power From on High

Another lesson which Elisha had to learn was that although he was a man of energy, a man who gave himself very thoroughly and fully and used up all his natural strength in what he did, his power was from on high. What we have said as to a man being diligent and in earnest, and putting all his strength into things, does not in any way contradict this, that even such a man has to learn, before he can move into his full spiritual usefulness, that the power for that is not in himself, but from on high. The Lord may take account of that man before, but even as it was with Paul with all his zeal and all his earnestness, he has to come to the place where all his strength is drawn from above, and not from himself. Elisha had to learn that it was power from on high, the Spirit sent down, that was the secret of strength. It is only so, that we shall be living testimonies. It is only so, that we shall be vessels of such a Testimony as this. (We are not speaking of the general kind of Christian work, we are speaking of the Lord having His fullness of Testimony in us. The fullness of the Lord's Testimony is the expression of the power of His resurrection in our very being, and for that there has to be a coming to the place where we know, in every realm of our being, that our strength is

not in ourselves, but in Him Who is above.) It is the One Who
has gone up to the right hand of God, Who is the Source of our
strength, the Spring of our energies; because He lives, we live;
by His power, and His power alone, we live and work. It is the
Lord in glory Who is our energy. Elisha learned that in type. For
all the future, his resource was the Spirit from above, the spirit
of his ascended master. That we have to learn in ever deepening
ways.

III. Having His Beginnings in Jordan

Finally, he had to come to the place where all his beginnings were at Jordan. The last step of that journey with Elijah,
and the first step of his journey under the Spirit, were at Jordan.
He went over with Elijah in death; he came back through Jordan
in the power of resurrection. The sons of the prophets, fifty men,
were watching, and as they saw him come back across the Jordan they said: "The spirit of Elijah doth rest on Elisha." His
beginnings, shall we say his roots, were in Jordan. We know that
there has to be a rooting in the Cross of the Lord Jesus, life having its very beginnings in the death and resurrection of Christ
experimentally known. Into the life of such an instrument of God
there has to come an experience which registers, once and for
all, that this life—in its good and its bad, in all its energies, even
for the work of God—has been brought to an end, so far as that
one is concerned. Even in Christian activities, and religious
interests, and passions for service, that life has been brought to
an end, and nothing is possible except in the power of His resurrection. It is one thing to say that, and to hold that as a teaching;
it is quite another thing to know that, and to have that registered
in your being every time you seek to move in relation to the
Lord; to know that every day of your life, so far as the Lord's
interests are concerned, you draw all from Him, that everything
is in the power of His resurrection, there is nothing else. To have
that settled, registered, established once and for all, demands a
deep Jordan experience. That is a deep death, a deep sinking into

Jordan, but that makes possible a wonderful Testimony to His risen life. That is the opening of the door to the vast, the ever-growing knowledge of Him in resurrection life.

Calvary closes the door on man by nature, but Calvary opens the door to the man who means that all is to be out from God and not from himself. Elisha came to the place where all his beginnings were in Jordan; every bit of His future was born in Jordan. You and I have to learn to be vessels of this Testimony; those who know Him in resurrection life.

That is preparation. If all who have gone out in the Lord's service had gone out on that basis, a very different story would have been told. We cannot hold ourselves responsible for all who have not, but what we can do is to recognize this to be the truth, and, so far as we are concerned, ask the Lord to make it true in our case. It is a deep death! This is an end, but also a beginning. What is before us is Testimony in what we are—not first by what we say—as to Him in resurrection life. If that is what is before us, that can only be on the ground that we ourselves have ceased in every realm of knowledge and of life which is not that; and that is the meaning of our union with Him in His Cross. This is preparation. This is equipment. This is where the Lord begins with His vessels for the fullness of His Testimony.

CHAPTER TWO

The Waters of Jericho

2 Kings ii. 19-22; Romans viii. 20-25, 1-2, 6.

While Elisha tarried at Jericho the men of the city came to him concerning the state of the waters, and the effect of that state upon all the fruit of the land, in that it fell before its time, and never came to perfection.

It is necessary for us, in order to get the full significance and value of this incident, to pass our eye over the history of Jericho in relation to the Lord's people up to this time. We remember the first encounter with Jericho on the part of the people of God, when the possession of the land was before them, and with our knowledge of that history, and of its details, we are able without any delay to gather it all up, and to recognize exactly what it all represents.

I. The Inclusive Representation of Calvary's Victory Over the Power of Satan Working Through the Flesh

The word "inclusive" is intended to bring us back to the recognition of the fact that everything which followed in the land was represented in Jericho. Jericho was, so to speak, the sign and token of everything. It gathered into itself the complete conquest of the land. The giving of Jericho, and the manner of the giving, to the people was God's token that He gave the whole land. We may call Jericho the firstfruits of the resurrection; and in the firstfruits the whole harvest is always gathered up representatively.

Seeing, then, that Jericho was the first issue of the crossing of Jordan, that is, the firstfruits of resurrection, you have everything that the Lord intends for His people, and which He has provided for them represented by Jericho. Thus Jericho is the inclusive representation of Calvary's victory, but of that victory as over the power of Satan operating through the flesh. For Jericho represents the strength of the flesh as energized by spiritual forces.

In studying Christ as the Inheritance of His people, the counterpart of the land of promise, we see that we only come into our heavenly position through conflict and conquest. The Ephesian position "in the heavenlies" is in relation to "principalities and powers, and world rulers of this darkness, and spiritual hosts of wickedness," and the fullness of Christ is only reached and maintained by warfare therewith. We know quite well that the instrument, the means of the forces of evil is the flesh as energized by them, and that Jordan most definitely represents, not merely victory over the enemy as the enemy, but victory over the enemy by the removal of his ground of advantage in the putting away of the body of the flesh. If it had been only a spiritual conflict, then it would have taken place altogether outside of the human realm, and man as such would not have been drawn into it. The incarnation, therefore, would have been without meaning. The spiritual forces of heaven could have met the spiritual forces of hell, and it would have been purely a spiritual conflict. But the fact that God was manifest in the flesh, to destroy the works of the devil, carries the battle into another realm, and shows that it is because the enemy has his power, and his advantage, through the flesh, that he must be destroyed in the flesh. The Lord Jesus took flesh, in order to destroy the works of the devil in flesh. So that Calvary's victory is over the power of Satan working through the flesh, and that is what Jericho represents.

Jericho

(a) Something Too Strong for Man

Here is something which is altogether beyond the power of man to deal with. When the spies went out in the first instance, the majority report was that the task was quite beyond their power. They saw cities great and walled up to heaven, and giants. Their report was that this was more than flesh and blood could contend with, an impossible proposition. And they were quite right, as far as they went. The trouble with them was that they did not leave room for the Lord.

The flesh is always that, and you have a parallel in the letter to the Romans; for when you read chapter vii. before you reach chapter viii., you know that you are up against Satanically-energized flesh, and every attempt of man to deal with that leads to the cry: "O wretched man that I am! who shall deliver me from the body of this death?" The whole of chapter vii. is a prolonged groan in the utter inability to deal with the flesh—"But I see another law in my members, warring against the law of my mind"; "The good that I would I do not: but the evil which I would not, that I do." That is flesh, not in the passive sense, but energized by an active law of sin and death, governed, of course, by the intelligent forces of evil. There is always that extra factor, and that extra factor is clearly recognized, inasmuch as the flesh has an uncanny way of trapping us just at the moment when we do not want it to, when it is least of all convenient for us to be caught by it. The whole thing is timed and planned with an intelligence that is uncanny, subtle, and watchful and is all related to other issues which are Divine, to frustrate them. It is not flesh that is just working automatically. It is a flesh that is energized by an intelligence. Jericho, then, speaks of Calvary's all-inclusive victory over the power of Satan operating through the flesh; something more than man can deal with.

(b) Fullness as Represented by "Seven"

The Lord commanded that the people should go round Jericho once a day for six days, and that on the seventh day they should go round seven times. "Seven" is always the number of completeness, comprehensiveness, spiritual perfection, so that in the very going round seven times is the Lord's illustrative way of saying that this thing represents the fullness and the conclusiveness of conquest.

(c) Achan

Further, the Achan factor is significant. There were two things connected with Achan's sin, or which were the forms of expression which that sin took. There was the wedge of gold, and the Babylonish garment.

The wedge of gold incidentally is of interest, inasmuch as it has been discovered that wedges of gold, not coins, formed the currency of that part of the world at that time. Business was transacted, and payments were made in this way, and, in a word, credit hung upon these wedges of gold. It was one of those wedges of gold representing the commercial values of this world which Achan took.

The Babylonish garment, on the other hand, is a foreign element, which has proved to have been a link with a religious system, the Babylonish religious system; for that Babylonish garment was nothing other than something connected with the system of worship in Babylon. It might have been a garment of a priestess.

The gold was claimed by Jehovah. When the city was taken it was commanded that the gold should be devoted to the Lord for His purposes; that is, the Lord laid claim to the gold, and all the gold was the Lord's property, the Lord's by right. Achan, therefore, appropriated what belonged to the Lord, and sought to turn it to his own account. That is what the flesh always does. The flesh always takes to itself the glory that belongs to the Lord. The flesh is always taking God's rights from Him. The flesh is always putting itself in the place of the Lord.

As to the Babylonish garment: that was a part of the whole system of things which was to be utterly destroyed *from* the Lord, and it represented a spiritual order which was in antagonism to God, a worship which was energized by the god of this world, his religious system, in usurping God's place as God; and that whole system, with every accompaniment, every feature, was to be utterly destroyed. But Achan preserved something which was a representation of a spiritual antagonism to God as the only God, so that Achan's sin was a very deep sin.

You see how inclusive Jericho was, in that its every feature foreshadowed, or represented, what the conquest of the land was to be. The judgment of Achan's sin showed that God had first rights, and the flesh must not appropriate what belongs to God, must not take God's place. It showed that the land represents a false spiritual system which had to be blotted out, and not one fragment of it left to survive. When Achan took the Babylonish garment he was violating a law which had to govern the conquest of the land, and he became the enemy's instrument of breaking into the Divine order, so that Jericho gathered up everything through the whole land. We are told in the book of the Acts that the Lord cast out seven nations greater than Israel. The "seven" of Jericho is symbolic of the seven nations which are to be destroyed, and they are virtually destroyed in Jericho.

Thus you have the flesh as energized by Satan, and Calvary's inclusive victory over the whole. That is what Jericho speaks of to begin with.

II. The Omnipotence of Faith in the Power of the Cross

It was all the work of faith. The going round once a day was a work of faith, so that day by day this march took place, and nothing seemed to be accomplished, no day seemed to close any nearer the ultimate issue than it commenced. At the end of six days, so far as any kind of human judgment could tell, nothing had been accomplished at all; they were no nearer conquest than they were when they started six days before. And then on the seventh day round they went, once, twice, thrice, four times, five times, six times, and no sign of anything happening. Faith is being drawn out to finality, to fullness of the seventh degree, the spiritual perfection of faith. And then, when faith has reached that point of completeness, it has to be expressed, has to be given a voice and a shout in the presence of a very great deal that would argue that it is all nonsense, all in vain, all foolishness. It would seem that there had been built up a tremendous amount of evidence that this whole thing is futile. And then in the presence of all that evidence, faith is called upon to shout victory. Faith is drawn out, extended, faith in the infinite value of the work of the Cross over all the power of the enemy. When faith reaches that point God comes in and vindicates Calvary. It is the omnipotence of faith in the power of the Cross that is represented by Jericho.

III. The Curse Resting Upon All the Satan-Energized Works of Achan

Joshua cursed Jericho, and Jericho became the representation of the curse resting upon all the Satan-energized works of man. It is very important to see that a curse rests upon all the Satan-energized works of man. That takes us right back to the Garden, and holds good through history. The features of that curse are two-fold:

(a) Death

Here you have an illustration of what spiritual death is. So far from being a ceasing to exist, it is something which goes on with tremendous activity. Spiritual death has many works, many activities, many energies put forth, and yet is lacking a vital something which justifies all those activities in the long run. The waters of Jericho lacked that essential element. Men labored, men spent themselves in the field; they cultivated, they tended, they watched over. They were successful up to a point. The result of their labors was seen up to a degree, and then everything stopped, and from that point there was no further progress, it failed.

(b) Vanity

That is the nature of spiritual death. It is what Paul calls "Vanity." It is work, labor, energy, but never going through to the fullness, to the finality, which God intended it to reach. Death and vanity! Vanity is the work of spiritual death. That is inevitably the nature of all works of the flesh, even though they be ostensibly for God. There will seem to be success up to a point, but no going beyond that; from that point no development. Yes, it is even possible in the flesh to produce something, to reach a certain point, and to have a certain measure of success, but if it is the activity of the flesh it gets just so far, and then fades out. It is the mark of a good deal that has been done in the Lord's Name. A great many activities have been entered into, a great deal of energy has been put into the work of God, a great deal of organized effort, and it looked as though there was a great result, and numbers have been noted, totals made, and reports given. And then years after you come to look for the fruit, and where is it? A great measure of it has come to naught. The work was for God; it was with the best of motives, but it was produced by man. It got so far, but it never went through. It is always so, and it is as important for the Lord's people to recognize that as it is for men out of Christ to know it. There is no possibility whatever of getting through on the level of the old creation. "The creation," Paul says, "was subjected to vanity." You cannot get away from that.

That is Jericho as you have it in the beginning. All that is carried over to Elisha. That history of Jericho is brought over to Elisha's day. It becomes necessary, therefore, for us to remind ourselves of what Elisha represents, and how he deals with this situation.

Elisha represents the power of resurrection. It is therefore significant that he has so much to do with death, and that the very first public thing that comes his way is his dealing with death along this line. He comes in in relation to the ascended Lord on resurrection ground.

Elisha's Roots Are in Jordan

All his beginnings were there. He stands, as it were, basically in Calvary, and that gives the main significance to his life and his ministry. He proved the power of victory over death when he took the mantle of Elijah, and smote the waters of the Jordan, and said: "Where is the Lord God of Elijah?" and the waters parted hither and thither, and he passed over. He proved the power of his risen Lord in the waters of Jordan, and it was in that power that he proceeded. His roots were in Jordan. In other words, the very foundation of his life was the power of the Cross.

If Paul is pre-eminently the New Testament example of that, it is equally clear that Paul had his roots in the Cross. If there is one Apostle who knows more than any other Apostle about the power of the Cross, it is Paul. He has seen this universal, mighty victory in every realm, and therefore he is the Apostle of resurrection life in a peculiar way.

Elisha's Power Is in Resurrection

Let us point out one meaning of that in particular. His power in resurrection was of this nature, that because of resurrection position he stood entirely outside of, and superior to the situation with which he had to deal. Resurrection always means that we are outside of the world. After His resurrection the Lord Jesus never again appeared to the world. He never manifested Himself personally to the world after His resurrection. The resurrection means that He had passed, in that sense, out from the world and stood apart, and His power over the world was His apartness from it. His ability to deal with the situation is because He is no longer involved in the situation. Resurrection life means that we are outside of the world spiritually, and in a superior position.

Elisha, therefore, could move in scenes of death without in any way being overcome by them, but being superior to them all the time, and handling them with absolute authority because he was in no way a part of them. His power lay in that.

We have to learn how to live by the power of Christ's resurrection, so that the death around us is not able so to impinge upon us as to bring us into its grip. Resurrection union with the Lord Jesus means that we are not involved in the death that is all around us. We can move in scenes of death and not be touched by death. This is a very important lesson to learn, how to be in life in the midst of death.

Elisha's Authority Is in Anointing

He had received the Spirit. We know that there is something unique about Elisha. He was the only prophet who was ever anointed. Kings were anointed; priests were anointed; prophets were *not* anointed. But Elisha is unique, alone. The Lord told Elijah to anoint Elisha to take his place. That carries its own meaning, because Elisha is a successor. That means that Elijah and Elisha are one man in two parts.

Carry that to the New Testament, and the antitype is Christ as the Head, and the Church, His Body, under one anointing. The Church is simply the vessel of Christ on the earth for the carrying on of His work in the power of the anointing. The value, the power, of the anointing of Elisha was made good on the ascension of Elijah to heaven.

Elisha has his authority by reason of that anointing. Anointing always implies that God is committing Himself, so that the authority of God rests where the anointing is.

Look at the little incident of the ridiculing of Elisha when there came out (unfortunate translation in our Version) little children and mocked him, saying: "Go up, thou bald head." The original has no idea of little children at all. It is the word that is used for young men, and it is also used for hooligans. Evidently this was a considerable band, for forty of them were mauled by the bears. It was a large company of young men who were out to mock the Lord's servant in view of the ascension of Elijah, and were, in effect, saying: "Just as Elijah went up, you go up!" mocking the rapture. There are plenty of people who are mocking the thought of the rapture today. But the point for the moment is this, that Elisha there and then exercised the authority which was resting upon him, in a judicial way, and cursed them, and there came out bears and tore them, so that a large number suffered under judgment. It was the Divine authority that was with him that came out there so distinctly. His authority was from above on the ground of resurrection and through the anointing.

Elisha's Vessel Is a New Cruse

None of those things can be true of the old creation: roots in Jordan; power in resurrection; authority in anointing. The exercise of all that, the going forth of all that spiritual life demands a new cruse. The new cruse is the new creation in Christ Jesus, which stands in this position, in this relationship to the Lord, with its foundations in the Cross, its life in resurrection, its authority by the Holy Spirit.

Elisha's Means Is Salt

Salt is a symbol of that which is incorruptible, and which stands in its incorruptibility against corruption, against death, challenging and dominating. That is nothing other than the resurrection life of the Lord Jesus standing as a mighty challenge to death, to corruption.

All that is summed up in Elisha, and all that, as gathered up into this man, is brought to the waters of Jericho. Is it not very evident that this man is a type of the power of Christ's resurrection, of life triumphant over death?

There is the type so fully, so richly set forth. But what is the spiritual value and spiritual application for ourselves? We turn to Romans viii., and see it there quite clearly. In those later verses, verses 20 to 25, we have the spiritual background of the life of the whole creation. The Apostle there says that the creation itself was subjected to vanity. That is a Divine act. There was a time when, because of certain things, the creation was deliberately made subject to vanity; that is, God put upon it a ban which was of this nature, that the creation should never realize its full end except on one ground. So that the whole creation is in the grip of that which means the impossibility of its reaching the end intended for it save only on one ground. The Apostle says that in parts of our being we are still involved in that. Our bodies are still involved in that. We groan within ourselves, waiting for our adoption, to wit, the redemption of our body. But he says that the creation—and ourselves as involved in the creation—was subjected to vanity *in hope*. It is not entirely hopeless, not *without* hope. But where is the hope? If the Lord Jesus has in His own representative Person gathered up the whole creation—for all things were created by Him, and *for* Him—and this creation, because of its rebellion, has departed from the purposes for which it was brought into being; if the Father gave Him that creation, and now it has failed, will the Father rob Him forever of the gift? No! He will subject it to vanity in hope. Now the Lord Jesus takes the creation representatively in His Own Person, and as man enters vicariously *into its state* and goes as far as to have the very curse resting upon it, made to rest upon Him. The very thorns upon His brow are symbols of the thorns and the briers which sprang up immediately God cursed the earth; and that curse is made typically to rest upon His Head. Then He dies as under the curse. The universal death is concentrated upon Him, and He dies as under a curse. When He is dead, where is the hope? Looking at Him naturally there is no hope; but God raised Him from the dead. That is where all the hope is. Paul says: ". . . in God which raiseth the dead." Christ raised from the dead is the hope, and the firstfruits of resurrection. The hope is in Christ risen. The hope is resurrection in Christ.

Read again Paul's great chapter, the fifteenth chapter of his first letter to the Corinthians, and you have the classic on the subject of what resurrection means. If the dead rise not, we are of all men most miserable: our preaching is vain: your faith is vain: ye are yet in your sins, without God, and without hope. "But now hath Christ been raised from the dead, the firstfruits of them that are asleep," and there is the hope.

Now note: Paul says we have the firstfruits. Though that is true, there are still realms in our being that are under this regime of vanity; our body is still subject to death. We have not the full redemption yet, but we have the firstfruits of the Spirit. We have resurrection life by the Spirit already in us. That is the firstfruits of the Spirit, the ground of hope. And because we have resurrection life already dwelling within, we have the guarantee that our bodies also will be raised.

What is the present good of that? "There is therefore now no condemnation . . ." no judgment, no curse, no lying under the Divine ban. "There is therefore now no condemnation to them that are in Christ Jesus. For the law of the Spirit of life in Christ Jesus made me free from the law of sin and of death." In the resurrection of the Lord Jesus we are delivered from the curse—that is, from the death which works vanity—and we have been brought into the place where we can go right through to the Divine end, the full realization that vanity no longer rests upon us. We are no longer held up; no longer in the position that we live and come to a point and that is the end, and we can go no further. We can go right on now! The fruit of life can come to perfection because the power of death in the curse has been cancelled in the power of His resurrection. The condemnation has been removed.

Apart from the great condemnation resting upon all men out of Christ, is it not true that when we allow ourselves to come under a spirit of condemnation from the enemy there is brought about an instant arrest, so that we can go no further, but stop short, and everything in our lives becomes blighted, and the fruit begins to fall? It is the effect of condemnation. The enemy is always trying to get children of God back on to a ground of condemnation in order to reverse the Testimony of His resurrection, and to spoil the fruit of union with Him on resurrection ground. The people who are not absolutely certain and settled as to their being on the ground of Romans viii. 1, are people who do not make very much progress; they get just so far, and there they stop, and their fruit falls before it ripens. That is to say, they are not people who can affirm with certainty and finality that "there is . . . no condemnation to them that are in Christ Jesus" or, to go further, that "the law of the Spirit of life in Christ Jesus made me free from the law of sin and of death." We have to live in the joy and the assurance of that, the certainty and the glory of that. The power of the enemy to spoil everything is destroyed when we see, that standing with our roots in the Cross of the Lord Jesus, and in the power of His resurrection, united with Him above by the Holy Spirit of anointing, we are no longer under condemnation, and there is no longer any reason whatever why we should not go right through to the fullness of Christ. When we recognize that, the enemy has lost his power.

We have pointed out before how great a change takes place between the verses that mark the close of chapter vii. and the opening of chapter viii. of the letter to the Romans, and the same change is to be noted in this second chapter of this second book of the Kings. Romans vii. may be called the chapter of the waters of Jericho—in death and vanity by reason of the curse; and it is a painful chapter. No goal is reached: nothing gets through; everything comes to arrest—"O wretched man. . . ." Chapter viii. opens the door to going right through in life. Why? Simply because chapter vii. is put in at this point by the Apostle to show the glory of chapter viii. as the outcome of chapter vi. Chapter vi. is Jordan. "For if we have become united with him by the likeness of his death, we shall be also by the likeness of his resurrection"; ". . . our old man was crucified with him, that the body of sin might be done away, that so we should no longer be in bondage to sin; for he that hath died is justified from sin. But if we died with Christ . . . we shall also live with him; knowing that Christ being raised from the dead dieth no more; death no more hath dominion over him." "Even so reckon ye also yourselves to be dead unto sin." Did Paul write what is termed chapter vii. at this point, in order to contradict all that, and to say that it is all theoretically true, but his own condition a complete denial of it? No! He writes chapter vii., to show what chapter vi. has dealt with. Chapter vii. is in fact the condition that has been dealt with by chapter vi. And then he says: Now you see, that condition having been dealt with, this is our true position because of chapter vi.—"There is therefore now no condemnation . . ."; "The law of the Spirit of life in Christ Jesus made me free from the law of sin and death." You cannot have chapters vii. and viii. together. For example, "But I see another law in my members, warring against the law of my mind . . ."; "For the good that I would I do not: but the evil which I would not, that I do" alongside of "There is . . . no condemnation." Paul is simply saying that chapter vi. is God's way of dealing with what is found in chapter vii., resulting in chapter viii. It is the power of His resurrection opening a clear way through, so that this hedged-up man in the arena, dragging around a dead body, has got his escape from that no-way-out life, that no-way-through life, into the open way that leads to the fullness of Christ, because he is on resurrection ground.

Christ is the Firstfruits of them that are asleep, and we have the Firstfruits. Therefore, we are linked with Christ as the Firstfruits in resurrection. And the firstfruits are always taken as a guarantee that the whole harvest will follow. The whole harvest that is going to follow is going to be a wonderful harvest, and has as a part of it the redemption of our bodies.

CHAPTER THREE

Elisha and the Sons of the Prophets

2 Kings ii.

In this chapter Elisha comes into view in relation to the sons of the prophets. They also are mentioned more than at any other time, and on quite a number of occasions they are in evidence in relation to him and his ministry. This has a significance which we must look into, and we should seek the Lord's help for an understanding of what this really means. Let us refer to a few passages:

2 Kings ii. 3, 5, 7, 55; iv. 38-41; vi. 5-7.

The Sons of the Prophets
Who and What They Were

We have to go back to the days of Samuel for our introduction to this particular form of the prophetic ministry. Originally the work which was afterward taken up by the prophets was done by the priests. It was the priestly function to instruct the people concerning the law and the ways of God. But in the days of the Judges the priests became so degenerated, and the priestly ministry fell to such a low level, that it became well-nigh extinct, and altogether inefficient and inadequate. Then Samuel came on the scene, himself doubtless a priest. With him there came a transition, and with him there came certain reforms. One of these was the instituting of these schools of the prophets, and we find reference made to one of them as existing at Ramah, with Samuel at the head. You will read about it in 1 Samuel xix.

We may say, what perhaps is hardly necessary, that the term, "sons of the prophets," must not be taken literally. It does not mean that these were sons of prophets, but young men of spiritual promise who were gathered together to be prepared for spiritual ministry. That preparation was along certain quite clearly defined lines, but mainly with one object. They were to be very thoroughly instructed and grounded in the law, especially the oral law as differing from the symbolic law.

The priestly instruction had been mainly along the lines of the symbolic law; that is, the priests taught rather by action than by word. What the priests *did* was the method of instruction originally. But that was symbolism and type, and therefore the people had largely to have discernment and perception. They had to be able to see through a symbolic act to a Divine meaning. When things were in a state of purity the people more or less understood the meaning of those priestly activities; they were able to see Divine thoughts as represented by outward acts. When things degenerated, as in the years of the Judges, spiritual perception and understanding almost entirely disappeared.

What we have as to the natural state of Eli typifies the spiritual state of the people. His eyes had waxed dim, so that he was almost entirely without sight, and he had become so weak, that he had no power whatever to control even the moral life of his own household. And that is a twofold representation of the spiritual state of the people under the priestly order at its end. Spiritual perception, insight, had so far departed and ceased that moral paralysis had set in, and government according to the mind of God had practically disappeared. Therefore, because spiritual insight and discernment (or what was called in those days "vision") had disappeared, a new form of instruction had become necessary, and that was the oral form. The prophets were trained, not by the symbolic or typical expression of the mind of God, but by the direct declaration of it in word. So that it was the oral law in which they were trained, to proclaim by word of mouth, and not merely by symbolic act, what the mind of the Lord was.

These schools of the prophets were set up with a view to preparing men to declare in a direct way the mind of God. There were other things which were associated with that, such as the spiritual history of their people, and of the world, from the Divine standpoint. Read the prophecies of Isaiah and Jeremiah, of Jonah, Haggai, and Daniel, and you will see how much there is of history, direct or indirect, which has been a studied thing. Daniel tells us he was made to know by books, and he mentions in particular his study of Jeremiah. He had come to a knowledge of things through those prophecies, and when you look at Jeremiah, you find that there is a good deal of history in his writing. So that an additional object for which the schools of the prophets came into being was the teaching of "spiritual history."

Then there was a further aspect of things bound up with these matters, which we might call spiritual patriotism. We emphasize the word "spiritual" since it indicates that God had chosen a people; that God had separated a people; that that people represented something for God in the midst of the nations, and that God was jealous over them because of what they represented for Him. Therefore the prophets were on fire with a holy jealousy that that people should fulfill its Divine vocation. That was the nature of their spiritual patriotism. They were jealous for Israel, because of Israel's Divine vocation. In the schools of the prophets, that which we call "ritual patriotism" seems to have been nurtured and cherished.

These were, shall we say, incidental, subsidiary matters in the schools of the prophets. The primary function was that which is the very essence of prophetic ministry, that is, the revelation of the mind of God by inspiration. Not revelation merely by study, by the deductions of the human mind, but revelation by inspiration; revealing the mind of God, because the mind of God had been revealed by the Spirit of God.

Thus the prophets stood as the instrument of Divine representation, the means by which God's thoughts, God's desires, God's will, should not only be proclaimed, but represented. The prophet should be not merely a spokesman, but the embodiment of the truth to be spoken. So we find that the Lord took the

prophets through experiences in which the very message
entrusted to them was brought out in their own hearts, so that
they should be not only spokesmen, but living representations of
the truth.

That brings us back to the schools of the prophets in
Elisha's day, and we see that they were for that purpose, to produce men who were representatives of the Divine thought in a
living way. You have there the starting point for the relationship
between Elisha and these sons of the prophets.

There is this further factor to be remembered that, so far as
the sons of the prophets were concerned as differing from the
prophets, they were in immaturity, and in a state of preparation;
hence the education which came by their relationship with
Elisha. You find in the passages to which we have referred all
the marks of immaturity in every case, and see what was necessary to bring them to the place where they could fulfill their
prophetic ministry and serve God.

That Which Elisha Represents

We must remind ourselves before going on of what Elisha
stands for. He represents the power of resurrection life, life triumphant over death, the full issue of the Cross. Elisha's roots
were in Jordan; that is where he began. So that what we expect
to find is that in his connection with these sons of the prophets in
their immaturity they are under instruction as to what is essential
in their ministry, and that that instruction is embodied in Elisha
himself; that is, that they will come to see that he has the indis-
pensable element for all ministry.

Take these first references to the sons of the prophets in
chapter ii., at Bethel and at Jericho. They said: "Knowest thou
that the Lord will take away thy master from thy head to day?"
Here we start with a very elementary thing, perhaps almost too
elementary to be mentioned, and yet something which it may be
necessary for one or another to take account of. We notice that
up to a point in this chapter Elisha is not honored by these sons

of the prophets, but they address him in a somewhat frivolous and flippant manner. He is regarded as a mere servant of Elijah, so that whenever they see the great master moving on, and Elisha with him, they thus flippantly say: "Knowest thou that the Lord will take away thy master from thy head to day?" He is simply the servant of Elijah, and their attitude, their manner, their speech, betrays some superiority in their thought of themselves.

Here is spiritual pride and conceit. They have little or no respect for this layman. They are sons of the prophets: they are in the way of the work of the Lord; they are "called to service." They have about them an atmosphere of what is official. This man has no office, other than recently having come to follow the mas.er, and wherever he goes the servant goes. That conveys to them nothing of spiritual meaning, so they regard him lightly. They have no knowledge whatever of his secret history with God. They have no perception at all as to what God was doing with him, and thus they take this superior, perhaps supercilious attitude.

That introduces what is a very elementary factor, but it is not an uncommon thing in the modern schools of the prophets. It is one of the perils of the institution, of having had a "call" to serve the Lord. Oh, the perils of a "call" to serve the Lord! Oh, the perils of a sense of having been chosen by the Lord! the perils of being mentally in a different category from those who have not so heard the call and been chosen! One of the marks, if not the hallmark, of spiritual immaturity is conceit, or pride. No one who has any measure of spiritual growth and development, is marked by spiritual pride. That is a very challenging statement. There may be an enormous amount of knowledge, all that the "schools" can impart, not only the special colleges, but the general schools of doctrine; there may be a very comprehensive grasp of the teaching of the Scriptures, and accompanying it spiritual pride and superiority, which regards others who have not come that way, who have not been through those schools, as something inferior. It does not matter how comprehensive, how great such knowledge may be, if there is a trace of that spiritual superiority, you may at once decide that that is immaturity. That does not represent any point of spiritual advance. Such people have yet to learn from the beginning. Let us ask the Lord continually to deliver us from spiritual pride, from superiority, from conceit. The word "conceit" simply means having the seat of things in yourself. We sometimes speak of "having the root of the matter in you." That phrase is used in rather a different sense. The opposite of conceit is of having everything in the Lord, and nothing in yourself; and that is spiritual growth.

The sons of the prophets then do not come before us in a very good light, but we must remember that they are in a state of immaturity and preparation, and we must rather take our warning from their example. God was doing something in Elisha. God had His hand upon Elisha. There was an inner history between Elisha and the Lord, and the Lord and Elisha, which no one else could see. The official people were entirely unable to discern that, therefore they misunderstood. Let us be careful that we do not ride roughshod over the exercises in other lives on the part of the Lord which are not manifest at present outwardly, because we think that we have something and are something. We never know but what something very deep is going on in a life which at present has not revealed anything so far as we can see of what the Lord is doing.

It is so true that anything in the nature of spiritual pride is a blinding thing. It paralyzes the optic spiritually, so that any kind of self-sufficiency makes it impossible for us to see what God is doing elsewhere. We can never see that the Lord is doing anything anywhere else, if we are so self-satisfied that the Lord is really bound up with us, and we are the beginning and the end of all the Lord's interests. Pride blinds, and pride dulls spiritual sensibilities. Elisha had good reason to feel very sore, had he been a smaller man than he was, because of the frivolous and flippant attitude of the sons of the prophets. But he was a big man, and his dealings with them later show that he bore no resentment. He really did live out that which he represented, a life which has no interests down here, but is a heavenly life, a life above.

We pass on to chapter ii. 7, after which follows Elijah's rapture, the mantle falling, and Elisha smiting the waters of Jordan and crying: "Where is the Lord God of Elijah?" the waters parting hither and thither, and Elisha passing through.

That brings us to verses 15-16. Here you have an advance, a good movement. There is now some recognition on the part of the sons of the prophets of Elisha, and of what God has done with him, and of the position in which God has placed him. Remember that Elisha stands for the power of resurrection, and although doubtless the sons of the prophets would not have put it in these words or understood it in this way, the spiritual explanation and interpretation of their action is this, that they recognized, accepted, and subjected themselves to the absolute preeminence of the power of resurrection in their lives. That is, they saw and they accepted that this was to be the governing thing in their own case, that for them all their life, their ministry, their future, was to be under the sway of Christ in resurrection. They were to fulfill their ministry in the power of His resurrection; they were to be subject to the risen Lord on the principle that resurrection life was to govern. That is the spiritual interpretation. That is the typical meaning of Elisha's position as here, and of the sons of the prophets, recognizing and accepting and subjecting themselves to that principle. *But* this is only in a formal and outward way for the time being; that is, what Elisha did really represent spiritually had not become an inwrought thing in its meaning and value.

To bring that to up-to-date experience and application, it simply means this, that there does come a point when we are confronted with a great fact, a comprehensive fact, a fact such as this, that all life, all ministry from this time onward has to be in the power of His resurrection, and in no other power—under the

absolute dominion, government, control of the risen Lord in His
risen life. That may be presented to us, and we see it, observe it,
take account of it, and say, Yes, it is true, I recognize that that is
the truth; I accept that, I surrender to that, I subject myself to
that. We mean it. We cannot get away from it. We cannot argue
around it. The thing for us as a truth is final. We are shut up to it.
It is not a thing against which we have any resentment. We see
that it is God's way for us, that God has appointed it, God means
that. And in a very honest, sincere way, like these sons of the
prophets, we bow to it, and we say to the great truth of Christ
risen, and of the government of His risen life from henceforth: I
submit myself to it, I yield myself to it, I accept that; henceforth
that is to be the pre-eminent principle in my life.

That is where the sons of the prophets came. That is where
we come. And yet there is all the difference between accepting a
position like that, and having its implications wrought into the
very substance of our being. We find that after this that thing had
to have a practical working into them, so as to be made real in
experience, and not only true in mind and general acceptance.

There again we are confronted with a challenge, because we
are so often brought up against the great facts and realities of
God's will, God's purpose, God's way, God's means, the
thoughts and desires of God as they affect our lives, and we find
ourselves shut up to it. It is as clear as it was to the sons of the
prophets that the spirit of Elijah did rest upon Elisha; and seeing
it thus, we bow to it, we accept it, we say: We will to be subject
to that henceforth. That is very good! That is a good step! It is
certainly a very big step in advance of the position in which we
found these sons of the prophets earlier in the chapter. But never
let us think that the acceptance of a position in our minds and in
our hearts means that we have come to the position. We may yet
have some way to go before that which we have accepted
becomes a reality. All the practical implications of that may yet
have to be wrought into us. The unfortunate thing with so many
is that they see the thing so clearly, it is so patent. There is no

argument, there is no question. It is true, it is final. Then they go off thinking that because they are convinced, even overwhelmed with the truth of it, that they have it, and they begin to talk about it, and preach it. They have seen something, but very often that thing begins to break down in their lives. They find that, while they embraced it with all their heart, the thing was not true in their experience, and they begin to get into trouble by the very thing that they have accepted. And because they go through experiences which, from the Divine standpoint, are intended to bring them experimentally to that position, but for the time being are so contrary to it, they very often say: "Well, this thing does not work. I was certain that it was right; there was no question in my mind about it, and even now I do not see anything else; but, so far as I am concerned, it does not work." And they get into confusion and contradiction, and then they abandon the whole thing. Others hold on in the midst of the mystery, and go through with God to a clear place.

It is as clear as anything can be that these sons of the prophets accepted something in a comprehensive way, and their acceptance was very genuine, but that did not mean that the implications had been wrought into their hearts. From the standpoint of God there has to be an acceptance like that; full, complete, honest, final: but then the Lord begins to apply that.

It is most significant, from the standpoint of spiritual history, that there is no break whatever between their acceptance of Elisha, their bowing to him, and then their beginning to argue with him, as you will see from verses 16 to 18. That is a contradiction of subjection, a denial of their accepting him as the governing principle of their lives. Immediately it is found that what has been in all honesty an accepted thing is not yet a thing which is a part of their being. Do you notice what is involved? If Elisha is the power of life triumphant over death, then he is up against features of death all the time, and this incident affords one example of making room for death by these sons of the prophets. Elijah had been taken by a whirlwind into heaven, and they argued:

". . . lest peradventure the spirit of the Lord hath taken him up, and cast him upon some mountain, or into some valley," making room for something far less than the utter and the ultimate thing. It is as though they said: "Well, after all, he may be lying dead somewhere."

There is a large scope for contemplation there, if we bring the matter into the realm of the New Testament, as to our failing to grasp the reality of Christ in heaven, the meaning of the Lord Jesus being at the right hand of God, and our falling below that, and all the death that is let in by such a failure to grasp, to apprehend its full value. But it is not our intention to explore that realm. We only mention it because there is a very big factor involved.

We keep to the simple line for our present purpose, pointing out, that here there was a making room for death by acting on the level of natural reason in spiritual things. Here was a great spiritual factor, which was embodied in the very man standing before these sons of the prophets. Elisha would never have been there as he was in that capacity, with that enduement, if Elijah had not gone into heaven. They were in the presence of the fact of the power of resurrection, and yet they must handle such spiritual magnitudes with the natural mind, and drag it down from its high level of heavenly reality on to the low level of human reasoning. They must verify spiritual things by their own natural minds.

That brings us back to Romans viii. 6: "For the mind of the flesh is death. . . ." These men were, after all, dwelling mentally in the realm of death, not in glory, ascension, rapture. They were not in the heavenlies in spirit. They were mentally dwelling in the realm of death. "Lest peradventure the spirit of the Lord hath taken him up, and cast him upon some mountain, or into some valley." That was their horizon, that was the realm in which they were living and thinking. And it was simply death, because it was the mind of the flesh.

We pass from Romans to Corinthians: "Now the natural man receiveth not the things of the Spirit of God: for they are foolishness unto him; and he cannot know them, because they are spiritually judged." That is death: and when we try to handle, analyze, pierce through heavenly and spiritual things with these minds of ours, this natural reasoning, we come to a deadlock, we come to an impasse, and we move in a realm of spiritual death.

These very men had seen what happened. They saw Jordan cleft; they had knowledge of the risen and ascended Lord, but they were not taking their own position in an experimental way upon it. They wanted to have a certain confirmation in the realm of sense. Oh! how the natural man longs to get confirmation through his senses. He longs to see something, feel something, to have evidences. Beloved, one of the marks of resurrection is that so often the whole thing goes on without any evidences in the realm of our senses. Do you think that the people who live in the power of His resurrection are always conscious of being simply overflowing with Divine life? Very often, like Paul, they feel as dead as anything can be in themselves, and yet the miracle is that there is that which is not of themselves enabling them unto the work, carrying them on. They are conscious of weakness, emptiness, dependence, and yet there is something of God which carries them on. If they were to stand still and say: "I am not going on any longer until I know in every part of my being, and in every factor of my life, the overflowing of His resurrection," they would not go on. The Lord does not meet us on that ground at all. These men showed immaturity by wanting evidences in the realm of the senses. Elisha shows how utterly he represents the principle of resurrection life by standing against all that is merely sentient. The flesh must have its proofs, and its evidences along its own line, but the spirit sees through and acts in another realm: "That which is born of the flesh is flesh;and that which is born of the Spirit is spirit."

So these sons of the prophets sought to take hold of resurrection life and draw it down to the limitations of man's doubts. If you and I do that, we shall fall out of the realm of that ministry and testimony to which the Lord calls us. It is a very great temptation all the way along to want evidences of the spiritual in the realm of our feelings and of our natural knowledge, instead of going on and knowing quite well that the going on is not by our own power; that it is impossible so far as we are concerned, and yet we are going on by reason of Him Who is our life.

Looked at naturally, all those who have known and lived on the principle of the risen life of the Lord Jesus would appear a very poor lot indeed. If you could gather all the men and the women of this New Testament dispensation who have lived wholly upon that principle of life triumphant over death, and you looked at them as men look at people, you would say: "That is a poor crowd." Take Paul! Some people would get a big surprise if they could see Paul as he was. We have all the romance of nearly two thousand years of the effect of Paul's ministry. We have all this volume of literature on Paul, his life, and letters, and work. If Paul were able to meet us as he was then, and we had no spiritual perception, but simply saw him as a man, we should say: "Is this the man who created all this literature, and caused all this talk, who has stirred the world to its very depths for nearly two thousand years? I do not see anything in him!" But there is a deeper side. So you ask him: "Paul, did you know all the way through your life, when you were in this great work, such resurrection power that you never had an ache or a pain, and never felt tired, and never knew what it was to be depressed, to feel fears, to be anxious?" He would answer: "I knew them all as few men have known them, fightings without and fears within. I knew what depression was; I knew what it was to be tempted to doubt; I knew what it was to go through dark patches where ultimate questions arose; I knew what it was to despair of life." We may take it that there were many, many occasions when Paul was not conscious pre-eminently of the power of His resurrection, and yet he was living on it, and that accounted for everything.

That which is real and that of which we are conscious may be two different things. All that we know at times is that we go on in spite of ourselves. What is it that carries us on? It is that other "something" that is deeper than thought, deeper than understanding, deeper than feeling; it is the Lord going on in us.

The sons of the prophets made room for death by opening the door for human evidence, proof through the senses. That is spiritual immaturity. They will never graduate to the full prophetic ministry, until that which is true of Elisha has become true of them. Let us recognize that if Elisha comes out of Jordan, has his roots in Calvary, and, therefore, is the embodiment of the meaning of the Cross, then for these sons of the prophets, and spiritually for us, he points to the absolute necessity for the natural mind going to the Cross before ever we can know the risen life in Christ. They would seek to be justified by their works, and so they scoured the mountains and the valleys. They would have been justified if they had taken the spiritual position and believed.

Turn to chapter iv. 38-45. Here we see that these sons of the prophets went out to gather herbs for a meal, and when they found some wild gourds and cast them into the pot, it almost meant disaster. The lesson is a simple and clear one. It is again the coming in of the element of death: ". . . there is death in the pot." Death comes in here amongst the sons of the prophets along the line of a lack of discrimination in what was suitable to the maintaining of the spiritual life. There is a dearth in the land, the very life of the Lord's people is endangered, imperiled. And so that which is necessary for the sustenance and maintenance of life is the primary issue. These men (note again) are in preparation for spiritual ministry, and one thing which will most certainly arise in their ministry, and a primary thing, will be the question of what is suitable for the spiritual life of the people of God. And the one thing that they will need in the fulfillment of that ministry is to have discrimination. Moreover, they are going to fulfill their ministry in times of sore need and pressure ; for the prophets came up, as we have seen, in connection with the state of spiritual declension. Prophetic ministry is to be exercised mainly in times when the order of God in its fullness and clearness is not obtaining, when things have swung away from the Lord's full thought, and the glory of the heavenly order is no longer existent. There will be, therefore, pressure and difficulty in the times when the prophets fulfill their ministry. The people will be in a state of great spiritual need, and the prophets will have to be in a position to say what it is that is suited to that need.

Pass your eye forward, and you will see the clash between the true and the false prophet. Certain false prophets prophesied the things which were pleasing for popularity's sake; things that they were expected to say; things that they would get reward for saying. And so they prophesied smooth things, and these things were death. The true prophet had to withstand the false, and prophesy the things which very often were not popular and acceptable. These sons of the prophets were preparing for their spiritual ministry, and that ministry was to be the ministry of life triumphant over death. And a great factor in such ministry is ability to discriminate between what is of life and what is of death, what is living and what is dead.

In this incident in the fourth chapter they go through a practical experience. They gather for their sustenance in a day of pressure, but they gather indiscriminately, and find that death is in the pot. When such a state exists, and there is pressure, it is so easy to mix things up. It is so easy to bring along something which really is not life because it looks all right. The devil is taking advantage of a time of spiritual famine today to get into the pot things that are poisonous and deadly. There is a great need today amongst the Lord's people. There is a dearth of real spiritual food, and with it a sense of need. The enemy is taking advantage of that sense of need, and unfortunately it is those instruments which have no spiritual discernment who are bringing in the thing which is deadly to the Lord's people. One of the marks of our day is a lack of discernment and perception, an incapacity for discriminating between the true and the false, when the false looks like the true. Wild grapes and wild gourds look so much alike. You can be easily deceived by appearances, and so they are all put in together. And today you notice the mixture of the false and the true, and that is the deadly element. There is the true there, but there is something else mixed in, and in the long run it is proved to be not life as it promised to be, but death, a deadly deception, a deadly contradiction, a deadly denial.

The whole point is that of the absolute necessity of spiritual understanding, by which spiritual discrimination is made as to what is suitable to a true spiritual life, and what is not suitable. You cannot feed what is of God upon something which is of man or of the world. It is unsuitable. That which is of God is a species which cannot thrive upon anything else but that which is of Him. If you feed it on anything else you introduce poison. We cannot live the risen life of the Lord upon anything other than what is of the Lord, and so Elisha cast meal into the pot. And what is the meal if it is not the Lord Jesus, the meal offering to God, God's absolute satisfaction with Christ? Prophets must always know what really is living food for the people of God. The sustenance of the Lord's people is by the impartation of Christ in His moral and spiritual excellencies.

Finally, in chapter vi., verses 5-7: "The place where we dwell with thee is too strait for us." The desire for extending the house may be quite a good one, we have nothing to say about that. The sons of the prophets take their axes and go down to obtain energetically the means for that extension. They enter upon a course of action for enlarging the house. And as they are felling the trees one man's axe-head comes off and falls into the water—the river Jordan. That is a calamity, but there are always lessons hidden in calamities. The elements here are those of energy, and the energy is represented by the axe. An axe is an energetic symbol. It speaks of strength in action. But this man who is the occasion of the story has a loose axe-head. His strength, his energy, is of an uncertain quantity and quality, and it fails to get through; it breaks down on the way. The parable is perfectly clear; we hardly need apply it. Here is good purpose, good intention, good motive, the object is quite commendable, but the initiative is with the man, and the energy is of man: and man's energy in the things of God is a very uncertain quantity, and sooner or later it will break down, and a state of death will exist, because that axe-head is at the bottom of *Jordan*.

May we stay for a moment and recall a further reference to the axe-head in another part of the Scripture. You will remember that the cities of refuge were appointed for the benefit of such as accidentally killed another man, and this illustration is given: The case is supposed of two men who went one day into the wood to cut down trees, and one man's axe-head came off and smote the other man, that he died. It is interesting that that is cited as an illustration of how a man may die accidentally. The city of refuge was provided for him who caused the death, that the avenger of blood should not take his life for the life of the one who has died. But we must remember that there is a certain responsibility for seeing that your axe-head is not loose. It is all very well to say that it was an accident, but what about the responsibility for seeing before you started that the head was on the axe securely? There is a moral principle involved there.

Here is a man who started out with a borrowed axe, and he never looked to see whether his axe-head was perfectly safe. That loose axe-head instead of going into the Jordan might have gone into another man's head, and the question of death would have been involved. In principle it is the same thing. Morally it is one thing. The axe-head is at the bottom of Jordan, and typically a state of death has come about because of an attempt—spiritually interpreted—to do spiritual things with natural energies.

We need say no more, other than to conclude the incident. The axe-head came back, and the work was finished, though now in the power of resurrection. But for Elisha being on the spot as the power of resurrection, as that which had conquered Jordan already, as that which had triumphed over death as represented by Jordan, that was the end of that man's work.

There are other features, but we will not touch upon them. We are simply taking what seems to be the heart of these things.

So we are brought to the fact that preparation for full use-fulness to the Lord in the power of resurrection means that we have to go through an experience where our energies are brought to an end, where the strength of the flesh is buried in Jordan, and where we can only go on because we discover the power of His resurrection.

With the seeking for the body of Elijah you have the natural mind at work. In the seeking for the food you have the natural heart at work. In the loss of the axe-head you have the natural will at work. Mind, heart and will, all having to pass through death, to come into the realm of the power of His resurrection.

So that Elisha's connection with the sons of the prophets is full of illumination. We shall miss the mark, if we just dwell with the typology. We simply use it, in order to get to the spiritual side of things. It would be quite easy for us to go to the New Testament and see this principle, and that principle, and the other principle laid down, but that would be but a statement made. We have preferred to go to the Old Testament and illustrate principles. The principles are in the New Testament as clearly as anything can be: for example, that the Cross does mean the end of the natural mind, so far as spiritual things are concerned: the Cross does mean that "they that are Christ's have crucified the flesh and the affections and desires thereof": the Cross does mean that the strength of "I" has to be crucified with Christ. But the Cross does mean also that in mind, heart, and will, the power of His resurrection has to be established, and can be.

While these sons of the prophets accepted the position in the beginning, it was only wrought into them stage by stage through experience, and each of those stages was simply the making real in them of the implications of their relationship to Elisha, what was bound up with him as being their head, their governing law of life.

We go through experiences to bring us there, but as we go through them we come to the place where we do know Him, and the power of His resurrection. The Lord teach us more fully what this means.

CHAPTER FOUR

The Nature of the Life and Testimony of the Lord's People

2 Kings iii and iv.

As we meditate on these chapters we must with every fresh step remind ourselves of the significance of Elisha himself. That is, that he came in on the ground of resurrection, to represent the nature of the life and the Testimony of the Lord's people. That was represented by the anointing, the coming of the spirit of his ascended master upon him, indicating that through Calvary, through the work of the Cross, he was in union with heaven in the power of resurrection, and everything that obtained in his life was in one form or another the expression of that resurrection life. Thus he came into touch with people and situations in various directions in the power of resurrection, and whatever Elisha touched was connected with the issue of life triumphant over death.

There are three things before us now, the details of which we shall not stay to deal with, but just be content with taking out the central thought.

I. The Valley Filled With Water

Resurrection Life in the Midst of Pressure From a Hostile World Outside

Chapter iii. is occupied with the rebellion, or revolt, of Moab against Israel. Probably you will recall that David had subdued the Moabites, and had put them under tribute to pay to Israel annually one hundred thousand sheep and lambs. That tribute had continued through the reign of Ahab. With the death of Ahab, Moab revolted. That revolt is mentioned right at the very beginning of this second book of Kings in the first verse of chapter i. There is then a break in the general history, in which Elijah is translated and Elisha comes into his place. It is interesting and significant that Elisha does come in right at that point.

If you get the larger background of spiritual interpretation in the light of the New Testament, what you have as represented by David is the Lord Jesus in absolute sovereignty, overcoming all spiritual enemies. You remember David went over the whole ground of every foe which had ever lifted itself against the Lord's people, and subdued them all, and established his throne upon a universal victory. That is typical of Christ by His Cross overcoming every spiritual foe. But then we find, not so long after the universal victory of the Cross spiritually established, the breaking out of hostile forces against the Church, seeming to be a contradiction to that victory, and yet not so in fact. Elisha typically is connected with the Church, and his ministry is to show and to bring in the power by which the Church is to know its life of victory in relation to the ascended Lord. That power is the power of resurrection life.

So we find that immediately upon Elisha's coming into his ministry, there is this revolt of Moab against Israel. Things are not in a very good condition amongst the Lord's people. Ahab has been responsible for a good deal of spiritual declension, weakness, contradiction. He has handed on a heritage of unfaithfulness, and things are at low ebb spiritually at this time. The alliance between Jehoshaphat, king of Judah, and the king of Israel in Samaria, is an unholy thing, a state of departure and weakness. That gives Elisha his real value. It clearly indicates why Elisha is brought in at this time. That is, the necessity is made very manifest by the situation.

The first lesson, therefore, that arises here for the Lord's people is the manner of establishing beyond any question the Testimony to the absolute Lordship of that One Who is at the right hand of God, in a day when in general things are spiritually at low ebb amongst themselves, and when from the outside world itself, as represented by Moab, there is severe pressure. How shall the Testimony of Christ's universal sovereignty be displayed? On what ground can it be maintained here? Elisha makes very clear to us by his own typical person what the Divinely employed means for that purpose is. It is a matter of conflict with the world in a day of inward weakness.

The situation becomes, as you see, very precarious. This designed resistance of Moab finds the Lord's people without the resources to carry it through. They move out, but they have no power by which to meet the situation. When they come to the actual moment of launching their assault they themselves are completely crippled and paralyzed by the lack of spiritual resource. The waters upon which they were counting did not exist; they had dried up. When these people came to the place where they expected to find the streams of water, those streams were not there, and the whole army was in peril of perishing for want of resource.

The issue is perfectly clear, and is stated by the king of Israel. This confederacy is going to perish, this whole situation is going to end in death, calamity, destruction. But Jehoshaphat, who represents the spiritual instinct in the situation—one who more than the others is in touch with God, who does know the Lord, has a relationship with Him—raises the question of consulting the Lord through his prophet: "Is there not here a prophet of the Lord. . . ?" This leads to a consultation with Elisha.

Elisha in the first place is moved by the unholy state of things. He refuses to have anything to do with the king of Israel, because of his unholy condition. Elisha seems to be inclined to turn the whole thing down; but then he remembers Jehoshaphat, and says: ". . . were it not that I regarded the presence of Jehoshaphat the king of Judah, I would not look toward thee, nor see thee." Wherever there is a true, a genuine looking in the direction of the Lord, the Lord does not despise that, nor refuse to take account of it. And so Elisha, taking Jehoshaphat into consideration, deeply and terribly moved by the evil of the situation, seeks to get detached from that side of things and says: "bring me a minstrel." Let us not be misguided by this to think that he sought inspiration through the minstrel. No such thing! He did not seek any soulish stimulus to get inspiration. Revelation from God does not come that way. Elisha had become terribly moved to wrath by the evil of the situation amongst the Lord's people, and it was quite impossible for him quietly to give the word of the Lord while he himself in his spirit was entangled in this thing. And the request for a minstrel was simply to get quiet in himself, to get his own spirit detached from this situation. You know that the quieting effect of the minstrel is mentioned on more than one occasion in different parts of the Scripture. Elisha disentangled himself from this situation, and then, in that detachment, was able to open himself to the Lord, and receive the Lord's Word. "Thus saith the Lord, make this valley full of trenches." We need not stay with all the details of this story; we note the central message.

Here we are in conflict with a hostile company, in conflict with forces which are bent upon the full and final destruction of the Lord's Testimony in His people, forces which are taking advantage of a day of general spiritual declension. In ourselves we have no resource with which to meet those forces, and that situation. How then will it be met? Upon what basis will the Testimony be maintained and brought out into fullness? Purely upon the basis of our knowing the Lord in a new way in the power of resurrection. It is a very simple lesson, but it is a thing which runs through the New Testament continuously.

You see it marking the life of the Apostle Paul again and again. You note the uprising of the hostile forces to quench the Testimony as represented by him, and a seeming advantage of those forces from time to time, so that the Lord's servant appears at times almost to be brought to a standstill. It does look as though the advantage is on the side of the enemy. And then, without any noise, without any sound of wind or seeing of rain, there is a reinforcing with the power of resurrection, and all the forces which have been ranged against the Testimony in him are scattered, confounded, and there is an establishment or a celebration of victory.

On one occasion those forces rose up and withstood the vessel of Testimony. It looked as though they had gained the advantage, that the enemy was in the place of power. The next thing you read is that Paul rose up and went back into the city, and at Lystra there was a great and abiding celebration of the power of resurrection as working in the Apostle. At Ephesus the same thing happened in another form—the rising up of the forces antagonistic to the Testimony, a riot, a driving out, and to all appearance the enemy in the place of strength. Nevertheless we have a letter to the Ephesians in which we have a great story of the establishment of the Ephesian assembly, and the Testimony there is of a very definite and positive form. And concerning Ephesus the Apostle said that it was there that he despaired of life. He was so sick as to despair of life. Ephesus, though as a church non-existent today, still moves in mighty power spiritually. We never read the letter to the Ephesians without recognizing how vital it is, and it has gone on in its spiritual persistence, in power and strength, for all these centuries. Eternity will reveal marvelous fruit from the battle for Ephesus which looked at times to be lost. The power by which the Testimony was established was the power of His resurrection.

What was true of Lystra and Ephesus was true in many other directions and on many other occasions. You see the rallying of the forces, a situation which appeared to be very precarious for the Testimony, and then, without any great noise, a rising up and a working of the power of the risen life of the Lord in the vessel, and a celebration of His victory. Instead of the vessel of Testimony being destroyed, that very life was the destruction of the forces which were set in opposition.

If you read this story in its details you will see that the thing which became the life of the Lord's people became the death of their enemies.

We are in that position today very truly. The full Testimony of the Lord is hard pressed. There is great profession, a great deal of Christian tradition, but the Testimony in reality is the Testimony to the power of resurrection in the life as a living thing within the saints. This is limited to a comparative few, and the pressure is tremendous upon that Testimony, to extinguish it altogether. The need is the need which is seen here—a fresh knowledge of the Lord in the power of His resurrection.

There are many remedies for the situation which are being suggested. Numerous Conferences are being held to discuss how the work of the Lord shall be brought into a better condition, and made more triumphant; as to how there can be more success, more effectiveness, and so on; and we are wearied to death of these Conferences, the discussions, the round tables, which issue in nothing. *The* need which touches the heart of the whole situation, and which will solve every problem, is a fresh knowledge of the Lord Himself in the power of His resurrection, a fresh experience of the risen life of the Lord Himself. There is no other means by which these spiritual problems will be solved, these spiritual deadlocks be removed. The only way is the uprising of the fullness of His life, and then the world will know. The Lord would say to His people today that, rather than for better ways and means, the need is for a life more mightily energized by that risen power of the exalted Head.

Elisha, who comes on the scene because he saw his master taken up into heaven and received a double portion of his spirit, forever tells us quite clearly that the Church's power in a day of declension and antagonism is the power of the risen ascended Lord. That is taking the heart out of the story. But let us remember that there had to be a real exercising of faith. The obedience of faith in the power of the ascended Lord became the victory which overcame the world.

II. The Widow's Oil

We pass on to the next incident in chapter iv. 1-7. The woman here was the widow of one of the sons of the prophets.

Inasmuch as the sons of the prophets were representative of those who were to be responsible for the Lord's interests amongst His people, but who were in a state of immaturity and preparation, we have the right background for what is here in this chapter as spiritually interpreted.

(a) The State of the Church
Unable To Meet Obligations

We find this widow of one of the sons of the prophets in a state of terrible impoverishment. She represents the spiritual state of the Lord's people, and that state is one of inability to meet the obligations. "Thy servant my husband is dead: and thou knowest that thy servant did fear the Lord: and the creditor is come to take unto him my two children to be bondmen." "I cannot face the creditor; I am not in a position to meet these demands; my two sons are going to be taken into bondage." Typically that means that the sons, who are types of the works, the fruit, of her life, are going to be taken over by the merely formal religious world. The Church is simply going to hand over its works, its fruit, and the world is going to take possession; the Church is going to lose all the value of its own activities.

(b) The Power of the World Over "the Church"

This is quite clearly the thing that is happening today. The world is using "the Church" for its own er '. It is the world that is getting gain out of "the Church" today, though not in a spiritual and right sense. "The Church" is in bondage to the world today. "The Church" is simply on its knees to the world. Every concert, every bazaar, every entertainment, everything like that in "the Church" is her unwonted, perhaps unintended, confession that it cannot live its own independent life. It is dependent upon the world for its very life. It says by these things, "It is no use trying to get on; we cannot maintain things even as they are, we cannot make ends meet, only as we recognize the claims of the world, recognize the strength of the world." Why do you provide entertainments and such things in your "Church" for your young people? Because you will never have your young people unless you do. They must have something of the world in order to hold them to "the Church" (so called), and thus "the Church" is slavishly in bondage to the world, on the knee to the world.

So the creditor comes to take and to despoil "the Church" of its real spiritual value. "The Church" is in a position where it cannot meet its obligations out from itself. It has not the spiritual resource with which to do so.

(c) A Little Oil

"The Church" has a little oil, like this widow. It is not altogether devoid of the Spirit, not absolutely and finally bereft of the Lord, but not by any means has it enough to stand up and live its own life independently of outside resources. To put that in another way, is to say that the fullness of life is not in itself, therefore it cannot face the demands made upon it. It has become an institution, enlarged by human effort, extended by man's organization, and therefore has become involved in the demands which are beyond its own spiritual growth. Its own spiritual growth has not kept pace with its external development. The life is not commensurate with what it has taken on, and attempted to do. That is the situation. That situation cries out, as through the voice of this woman: "There cried a certain woman. . . ." It is a pathetic position.

What is the remedy? It is the same remedy, only applied in another direction. It is Elisha, to begin with, the power of resurrection again, the risen life of the Lord, the full issue of the work of the Cross in absolute ascendency over spiritual death. Thus Elisha comes into touch with the situation. Here we see that *the* need in all such times of spiritual inability to meet spiritual demands, is a fresh knowledge of the Lord in the fullness of His risen life.

It will work at one time as to the pressure of the world from without in its antagonism, as represented by Moab. At another time it will be expressed by reason of the inward impoverishment of the Lord's people to meet the demands which are legitimately laid upon them. Paul recognized those demands and did not say that they were wrong. "I am debtor" he said, "both to Greeks and to Barbarians. . . ." He was under obligation to meet the spiritual needs of all men. But the spiritual needs of the world can only be met as we know the fullness of the risen life of the Lord.

"What hast thou in the house?" "Thine handmaid hath not any thing in the house, save a pot of oil." "Go, borrow thee vessels . . . not a few." You notice that in every one of these movements for renewal (revival, if you like), the knowing again of the Lord in the power of His resurrection, there is a challenge to faith. "Make this valley full of trenches." See these men, with no sign whatever that there would be any rain, with no idea whatever as to where water could come from, yet in obedience digging away and making the valley full of trenches. Their part was the obedience of faith. They had to leave the rest with the faithfulness of God. "Go, borrow vessels. . . ." The natural man would have reacted to such a suggestion with the question, But where is the oil coming from for the vessels? I do not see how it can be done! That is always the attitude of nature; wanting first of all a demonstration to the senses before it will act. God's principle is the obedience of faith. "Go, borrow vessels abroad of all thy neighbours. . . ." But what will the neighbors say? They will laugh at me! Nevertheless obedience of faith often involves us in situations which to the world are very ridiculous. Such obedience involved Abraham in what looked like a very ridiculous situation: "Now the Lord said unto Abram, Get thee out of thy country, and from thy kindred . . . unto the land that I will show thee," ". . . and he went out, not knowing whither he went." To all inquiries as to where he was going he would have to answer: "I do not know." How ridiculous that would appear to the world! However, that is just where faith has its real value, in that it is prepared to move, not caring what other people think, but trusting God.

How are these obligations going to be met? The means will be the risen life of the Lord. First of all it will necessitate stepping out in faith on the Lord's Word. Then it will involve putting into operation the little that you have of the Lord. Do you know the Lord in a little measure? Have you the one pot of oil? Put it into operation in faith? So many of the Lord's people are wanting to know a great deal more of Him before they will move at all. They have just a little knowledge of the Lord, and the Lord's principle is that there is never any increase until we have extended to the full what we have. Have you some little knowledge of the Lord? Well, extend it to the full, and act in faith in relation to it, and you will find your increase comes that way. Believe that this life in God is a fullness of life, although your measure of it at present may be very limited. It is not the measure we have that is the ground of expectation, but that from which we received what we already have. It is the fullness, of which we have received perhaps only a small measure, that should be our confidence.

If the woman had simply fixed her attention upon that one pot of oil, and said: "That is the beginning and the end of all my hope and expectation," then nothing would have happened. But she had to see that vessel in relation to a fullness which was boundless. If you take your little as the all, you will not get very far, but if you relate your little to God's all, you can go on. It is His fullness, not just the measure that we have experienced of His fullness. The fullness of God is a fact lying beyond our present experience, but a fact concerning which we have to act in faith.

That action of faith demanded on the part of this woman the bringing of vessels. Those who have ministry in the Word know quite well of what we are speaking: for example, that you do not stop gathering the Lord's people together because you feel empty. In the consciousness of emptiness, weakness, smallness of resource, you go on, and you find the Lord meets the need as you go on in faith. If at times we were to act according to our own feelings we would say: "We will not have a meeting today, we have nothing to give." But the Lord is our Resource, and as we go on the Lord comes in and fills the emptiness. It is a sound principle for the Lord's servants to work upon. If we are in the way of the Lord's Testimony we can trust the Lord to meet all the need, though we may have a very small measure consciously at any given moment. Do we believe that the Lord can meet the need, and fill wherever that need exists? There is no need represented in this world which, if brought before the Lord, cannot be met. If you have any doubt about that, there the Testimony stops. The point where you cease to believe a situation to be capable of solution by the Lord is the point where your Testimony fails; you are contradicting the power of His resurrection. The power of the risen life of the Lord Jesus is without limit, and there is no situation and no life which truly represents a need of Him which cannot be met.

For this woman it was a case of keeping on keeping on! She set the limit, not the Lord. When she ceased to find vessels then the oil stayed. The limit is not on the Lord's side.

The Testimony is along those lines. There will be differing ways of application. You and I will know how it touches us and our situation. From time to time we shall find that this applies to the position in which we find ourselves. It would be quite impossible for us to cover all the ground of application, but here is a fact stated. It is the power of His resurrection which meets the obligations; not what we have but what He is; not the measure of what we have already received, but the measure of what there is yet to receive. The Lord's thought for us is fullness, but we shall not have it all at one time. His fullness will come to us progressively. We shall not always be living in the consciousness of being full, but we can live continually in the knowledge of being filled again and again as the demand arises.

III. The Shunammite's Son

Let us turn to the latter half of chapter iv., verses 8-37. We want to condense this into as concrete a thought as possible. There is a change here which is somewhat significant.

In the case of the wife of the son of the prophets we have a woman manifestly in poverty, in emptiness, in privation, and the oil brings to her fullness in her emptiness. When we come to this woman of Shunem we find that we meet quite another situation. She is called "a great woman." That means that, so far as temporal matters were concerned, she was well provided for; in comfort, in plenty, in affluence, in position; just the opposite of the other woman. Unlike the widow of Zarephath, to whom Elijah went and whom he sought to persuade to give him something to eat, this woman has to try to persuade the prophet to eat. It is quite the other way round. She has plenty in every way but one thing. The prophet contemplates this woman. He looks at her home, her table, her servants, her possessions generally, and does not see anything about her home that is lacking, and for him it is quite a problem how to enrich her. The needs are not obvious; it is something to cause consideration. What can be done for a woman like that? Gehazi touches the vital spot: "Verily she hath no son. . . ." A deeper depth is touched. Everything *but* the one thing which can really mean more than everything else. One thing representing more than all these outward things. That fact is disclosed by the prophet's word concerning the son. The woman replied, "Do not lie unto thine handmaid." That seems to say: "There is one desire of my life, but it is impossible, and I have had to settle once and for all that that cannot be. I have fought my battle: I have accepted the denial; and now that is a closed door. Do not begin to bring me into a realm where that whole thing is raised again, and I have to fight my battles all over anew. Do not suggest things that, should they never come to pass, would put me back again into a place where all that I have means nothing to me because of that lack!" Nevertheless the prophet's word comes to pass, and from that time all things are swung over to this son. Then ". . . it fell on a day, that he went out to his father to the reapers. And he said unto his father, My head, my head. And he said to his servant, Carry him to his mother. And when he had taken him, and brought him to his mother, he sat on her knees till noon, and then died." She took him and laid him on the prophet's bed and went for the prophet. You know the rest of the story.

The Supreme Need: Fullness of Resurrection Life

What is it that comes out as the central reality, the thing which is the *supreme* factor in life? (There may be many other things. There may be a condition such as was found in one of the Churches in Asia to which the Lord addressed these words: "Thou sayest, I am rich and increased with goods, and have need of nothing; and knowest not that thou art wretched and miserable and poor and blind and naked!" There is a lack which by its very existence makes all else that you have as mere poverty. You may have all this, but the absence of one thing makes it plain that you have really no heart in all that.) The thing which counts above all things is to know within our own being the power of His resurrection. We may have much that is good externally, even in a religious way, but the one thing upon which the Lord puts His finger as the primary, the paramount thing in the life of any child of His, is not the abundance of the things possessed, but the knowing of Him and the power of His resurrection.

Look at Philippians iii. Paul there goes over all the things which were of value, which men would value and regard as things worth having. Then he sums them all up and says: "I count these, after all, great as they are in the eyes of men, as utter refuse, and suffer the loss of all things that I may know Him, and the power of His resurrection." This woman came to know this thing in a very deep way. The son was given; that was wonder enough! And yet there might still linger some suggestion that nature had had something to do with it, that the gift of the son could somehow be accounted for along natural lines. (Psychology has tended to undermine the whole realm of the objective and exclusive activity of God.) But God is going to demonstrate that this was wholly outside the realm of nature: and so the son dies, and is brought back to life, and every question of nature having a hand in it has been silenced. There is no room for anything natural when it is a case of resurrection from the dead. That is the ultimate Testimony. That cannot be explained in any other way than "God"! Resurrection is knowing God. Psychology tries to explain a good many things in Christian experience, and some of us have had much painful experience over the psychological explanation of religious experience. But the Lord has put us outside of that realm by making us know something for which psychology can never give an explanation, even the knowing of "him, and the power of his resurrection." Psychology cannot raise the dead. There is an inner secret history of knowing the Lord in a way that cannot be accounted for on any other basis than the power of His resurrection.

That is where the Testimony reaches its final point. It is the Testimony that Jesus was raised from the dead. That may be but the basis of the Testimony, but it is not merely the creed, the doctrine, it is the inward knowledge of the risen Lord. That had to be wrought in principle into the very being of this woman, until it was beyond the reach of any question. What was the full thought? It was Sonship. Read Romans viii. and Galatians, and see what sonship is when brought through into its fullest meaning. When the child was born, that represented what the New Testament has to say about our being children of God by birth. When the son was raised, that represented what the New Testament has to say about sonship by resurrection. The New Testament teaches by its two distinct Greek words that by our new birth we are children of God, but that sonship is something in advance of childhood. It is childhood brought to maturity in the power of resurrection. "Adoption" is the word used, as we know. But in the New Testament adoption has nothing to do with the taking into the family of an outsider. It has only to do with the adopting of your own child at his majority in the place of honor and responsibility. The Greek father adopted his own son when his son came to his majority, and that was the moment when he ceased to be a child and became a son. That is the New Testament teaching.

Here is the woman who had the child, and that is wonderful. When we are born again it is a miracle, a glorious thing. But when the Lord takes us through experiences to bring us to know Him in the power of His resurrection in our very being (not something done outside of ourselves, but something which has been done in us), and we are taken through deep depths, until in our very being we come to know Him and the power of His resurrection, that is sonship, that is the Testimony. The Testimony in its fullness is not bound up with spiritual infants, it is bound up with spiritual maturity. This woman was great, and yet there was a "but"! We may have a great deal, even in our Christian lives and in our Christian work, and yet there may remain that "but." There may be so much of it external, on the surface. The necessity is that that shall come right down into the depths of our inner being, so that we know Him in the very substance of our being as the Resurrection, and the Life.

It is only as the Lord's people come to that position that they are constituted a vessel of His full Testimony, and that explains why He takes us now, as His children, through the depths, that we may so learn to know Him.

Whatever the direction the principle remains the same, whether for conflict, as with the hostile forces around, or service, in the meeting of our obligations, or in life, the coming to the fullness of the Lord's thought. The one governing law is "Him and the power of His resurrection"; knowing the risen life of the Lord.

CHAPTER FIVE

The Healing of Naaman

2 Kings v.

While, strictly speaking, this incident has its place within the realm of the salvation of the sinner, it has general principles of a wider scope and fuller application, and therefore becomes a matter for the serious consideration of the Lord's own people.

Let us remind ourselves, at this point, of the position typically represented by Elisha. It is not a study of the life of Elisha, nor of a book of the Bible with which we are occupied, but a seeking to know the Lord in the power of His resurrection. The power and fullness of resurrection life is what gives meaning to the life and ministry of Elisha.

The Natural Man

Naaman is a representation of the natural man, as he is outwardly, and as he is inwardly.

Naaman is said to have been a great man before his master, a man held in honor, a man of reputation, of position, of ability; a man of success in his own realm. And yet, with all that can be said for him as to his greatness, his reputation, position, ability, success, death is working in him. There is one thing set over against all the rest, which casts a shadow over it, and brings it all into a realm of death. Death is active, death is working, death is the master of the situation, and, therefore, all else is under the reign of vanity; that is, everything is subject to a lease, and can at best only go on for a while. It will all pass, unless something happens. That is the man presented, the man by nature.

Then he is brought into the realm of things Divine. Initiative in the matter is taken apart from himself, outside of himself.

He is not the first one to move. The little serving maid of his wife is the instrument by which the link is made between him and the source of life. Sometimes quite small things become the means in the hands of God of bringing about such a link. Insignificant things, humanly speaking, are often used; and it is a thing to note in this story how the Lord's means and methods are of a different character altogether from those which Naaman would have considered suitable to his case. Grace very often moves for our good through means which we would hardly take account of, things which do not bear any mark of reputation whatever.

Through this simple, and, so to speak, insignificant (it proved to be a very significant) instrumentality, Naaman is brought within the compass of the ministry of life. It looked like a chance thing. The thing seems to be so unarranged, so like a chance expression. This little serving maid said to her mistress: "Would God my lord were with the prophet that is in Samaria! then would he recover him of his leprosy." It is little more than a sympathetic ejaculation—"I do wish that you could get into touch with such-and-such a means that the Lord uses!" And within a hint, a mere suggestion, there is the working of a Divine energy with tremendous issues involved.

Men organize great movements, and bring a good deal of pressure upon people as to why they should attend such-and-such a thing. The Lord very often effects His great ends in much more simple ways, which look to be merely accidental, incidental, at times. There is a wonderful simplicity and quietness about the ways in which the Lord gets His main ends. They just come about. A suggestion, a hint, an indication, an intimation, but lying in the direction of that there may be the ultimate things in the will of God.

This thing was never planned, never worked out beforehand, never elaborately arranged. In a very simple way, it just came about. It is something to take account of, lest the very simplicity of the ways of the Lord should catch us in an unwatchful state, and because we expected some voice from heaven, or some far more imposing method of God to get us into His full purpose, we miss those simple movements of life which were pointing in that direction. What a great deal hangs upon this very simple heart-expression of this maid!

Out of that Naaman eventually comes into direct touch with the instrument, the vessel of life—life in its fullness, life which was to triumph over death at work in him. But then his real difficulties commence. It is not until he comes into touch with life itself that the real state of the man is made plain. He knows he is a leper; that is, he knows that despite everything he possesses there is a serious lack, and that unless that lack is made good life for him is after all a disappointing thing, and could never satisfy him; everything has a shadow over it because of that one lack. In reality, however, the true character of the man's whole condition is not disclosed until he comes directly into touch with the means of his deliverance, when another kind of history commences, which really illustrates for us the nature of the natural man, even at his best.

Embodying it all in one comprehensive statement, his difficulties are the acceptance of the full implications of the Cross. He can accept the fact that he is seriously in need. He can accept the fact that his need might very well be met in a certain direction, and is prepared to go so far in that direction to have his need met. But then he comes up against the full implications of what that direction means, and he finds himself at that point unable to accept all the implications. Being the natural man, he requires some recognition of his own qualities. He needs to have himself taken into account in his own person. He is a man with a reputation, held in honor, and therefore he ought to be dealt with by quite reputable means, something quite in keeping with his standing. Thus when it is proposed that he should adopt means, and go by a way which to him, from his standpoint, was quite disreputable, he finds himself confronted with what Paul calls "the offence of the cross." "Are not Abanah and Pharpar, the

rivers of Damascus, better than all the waters of Israel? may I
not wash in them and, be clean?" Something with a reputation,
something more suitable to such a one as I am! And that is the
root of his trouble.

That can be applied in many ways, and various people come
up against the same deadlock along different lines. For some it is
intellectual; they must have an intellectual salvation, and if they
cannot bring everything into the realm of their intellect then the
thing is not worth considering, it is beneath them. Others must
have it in other vessels, and by other means which are suitable to
them in nature. But, be it what it may, God has His own position
as represented by the Cross, and God never deviates one hair's-
breadth from that. God's ground is utter self-emptying. That is
the Cross! When we come to Jordan, that means that we have
come to the place where all consideration for reputation, position, honor, or any such thing in the realm of the natural man has
been fully set aside, and we can never come to Jordan until that
is so. Naaman may have his battle, just as multitudes of others
have had their battles, on exactly the same ground, until they
could get through to the place where no consideration whatever
for themselves, as being anything of any value at all, has a place.
If the waters of Jordan remain symbolic of Divine judgment of
man, then that puts man down into a very low place, that reduces
man to something without a reputation, without honor. There can
be no getting through to the Lord's fullness of life, only insofar
as man by nature has been emptied out to where he no longer
regards himself as being of any account before God.

These are simple truths, but they apply to believers as much
as to unbelievers. The full implications of the Cross have not
been kept clearly before the Lord's people through the ages.
Unfortunately a great deal of Gospel preaching has laid all the
stress upon the satisfaction of man, the good and the blessing of
man, with the result that afterward, sometimes years afterward,
the Lord has to bring home the fact of the Cross as ruling out
man by nature. The consequence has been that we have had to

have conventions and special meetings to get Christians conse-
crated; and consecration is really a matter of full surrender. But
what an obvious fault that is, when all that should have been
done right at the beginning without any reservation at all. And
had the Cross in its full implications been presented right from
the beginning, then the believer would be living on the level of
the convention life from the first. We have all suffered from the
fault. Most of us, or many of us, have spent years in floundering
along in a large measure of weakness and ineffectiveness,
because we had never from the beginning seen the full implications of the Cross as to ourselves. We saw that Calvary was salvation for the sinner, but we had never seen clearly that Calvary
was the setting aside of man utterly in himself; and it was not
until we came to see that, that we came through into the fullness
of life. We had brought over a very great deal of our natural life
on to new creation ground, and, having tried to use it, we found
that it was a constant burden and handicap, whereas the meaning
of the Cross is that all things are of God. That is a comprehensive and conclusive "all." All things are out from God.

For Naaman the full implications of the Cross were presented, and not one bit of consideration was given to his flesh. No
provision was made whatever for his flesh. He came with his
pomp and retinue to the tent of Elisha, and sent to announce his
arrival, but the prophet did not so much as rise from his stool to
look out and see what wonderful man this was. He simply went
on with whatever he was doing, and said: "Go, and wash in Jordan seven times. . . ." The man of reputation felt the sting of the
ignoring of *himself,* and he was going away in a great rage, saying: "Behold, I thought, he will surely come out to me, and stand,
and call on the name of the Lord his God, and wave his hand over
the place, and recover the leper." Elisha's attitude was: "Not in
the least! that is the measure in which I respect the flesh!" That is
the measure in which God takes account of man by nature!

It is a painful lesson for a great many servants of the Lord
to learn. Not in the least does the Lord take account of what a

man is in himself; not even as to what a saved man is in himself. That man does not come under the eye of God. The prophet would not even look out to see Naaman. That is God's attitude. The eye of God does not take into view what man is by nature; He simply ignores him and sets him aside. Calvary represents that.

It is the way of life, the way of fullness. It seems to be very much the opposite when you are going through those stages, when those principles are being applied. There seems to be no life at all in that direction, and little hope. It is quite true! The natural man may as well take it for granted that there is nothing for him in that direction, as the natural man. Our flesh will get nothing out of salvation when God has His way. Our natural life is not going to get any gratification. Taking up the Cross and denying ourselves is something of a very radical character when wrought out in spiritual terms. It is self *denial!*

That is the meaning of Calvary, and such a presentation discovered Naaman's real heart state, and illustrates for us what death is. Death working is, after all, only the working of the natural life. To men it may appear a great thing. There may be that about it which man would call honorable. It may have a good deal of success in this world. There may be features of great ability. There may be a good reputation amongst men. But before God there is something else which renders all that as nothing, not to be taken into account; it is the reign of spiritual death. Naaman was put to a very thorough test as to whether he really meant business in this matter of resurrection life, life triumphant over death. He was fully extended as to whether to him this was a matter of life and death. "Go, and wash in Jordan seven times." The meaning of "seven" is spiritual completeness. Naaman was being drawn out to a point of spiritual completeness.

The story has nothing to say about Naaman stopping short after the second, the third, or the fourth time, and this shows that now he was really going right through with this whole thing, having once definitely faced the issue. His servants had reasoned

with him, and he had listened to reason. Then confronted with
the issue, he said in effect: "Well, if this is the way, then I am
going this way without any reservation. My alternative is to go
back to my country as I came, in this living death. Am I prepared
for that? or am I really prepared to go all the way with this matter without a reservation?" He decided, because of the serious-
ness of the issue, that he would go all the way. And so, although
on any other ground of a less complete consecration he might
have stopped after the second dip in Jordan, and said: "Well,
there you are! Nothing has happened! Just as I expected!" we
find instead that Naaman persevered. And now the third time,
nothing! The fourth time, nothing! The fifth time, nothing! The
sixth time, nothing! But he went through to the seventh time. His
faith was tried on this matter right up to the end.

We know what that means in our own experience. God has
placed before us an issue. That issue is no less a thing than life
triumphant over death. That not only applies to the unsaved, that
applies to saints. The full expression of that life was seen by the
Apostle Paul to be bound up with a certain point of advance-
ment, when he said: "Not that I have already obtained, or am
already made perfect . . . but one thing I do, forgetting the things
which are behind. . . . I press on toward the goal unto the prize of
the upward calling of God in Christ Jesus." "*If by any means* I
may attain unto the resurrection [Greek—out-resurrection] from
the dead," a resurrection which is a reward, and not a resurrection which is a general thing ; some expression of the power of
His resurrection which is not general but specific. So that you
see the matter of life triumphant over death in its full meaning is
something which concerns saints after Paul's type, and goes a
long way on into the Christian life and experience. But beyond
the initial expression of His resurrection in our salvation, and the
ultimate full expression in the out-resurrection from the dead,
there are continuous crises, progressive developments of that
life, and each fresh stage issuing in further fullness is marked by
some crisis of this very character, namely, as to how much more

of self we are prepared to leave behind. It may be that at a given point our own personal will is set against the Lord's will, or that a form of sin is present that we are not prepared to give up. On the other hand it may not be in the realm of definite and positive selfishness, but there are points of a fine character to which we come in the matter of our preparedness to let go something, some position, some relationship, and move on with the Lord into a new realm which is costly, and which means the setting aside in a new way of our own sensibilities, and our own feelings, and our own ideas, in order to attain unto that fuller power of His resurrection. We shall be challenged by these things continually as we go on, and for us the power of His resurrection is bound up with the extending of our faith to some further point than ever before.

That is the statement of facts. We shall know that that is true, if we are going on with the Lord, and perhaps the value of what is before us now will be found in our being able to say, when we come to such issues, and such crises: "This is just that: the question for the moment is whether I am prepared to take this further step, which, involving me perhaps in further difficulties, means that my own personal considerations have to be set aside in a new way." Thus it is a step of faith more than ever before. But it is the way of life, the way of increase. Naaman went the whole way with God, and God went the whole way with him, even unto the seventh degree.

After the seventh time Naaman came again whole, not only of his leprosy, but with his flesh as the flesh of a little child. It is not only that the positive action of death has been removed, but he has come into a new realm altogether. The flesh of a little child speaks of entire newness, a new life, a new realm. For him, speaking typically, it was like beginning life all over again as a babe; everything was before him. A whole new world was stretched in front of him.

That is the spiritual effect of every fresh breaking through into resurrection life. Every time we are touched with some fresh experience of His life we are conscious that it is a new world. There are new possibilities. The limitations of the past have become as nothing in the fresh possibilities which have come to us on the ground of this measure of risen life. It is always like that. There we reach the point of newness of life in possession. What remains is simply the expression of that newness of life in certain directions.

A New Attitude Toward the Instrument Used for His Spiritual Good

Naaman was very angry with Elisha beforehand. He would go away in a rage. But now he came to Elisha. There is no question of reputation now, of personal importance now. He made his way instantly and directly to the tent of Elisha. He sought fellowship with the instrument of blessing. He was no longer ashamed of that.

You can make the broad application of the principle of fellowship being established in life, because life shared is the basis of fellowship, and when once we really share some life we have the foundations of fellowship, and all dividing elements are put away.

Naaman Worshiped Jehovah

He worshiped Jehovah and said: "Behold now, I know that there is no God in all the earth, but in Israel." It is a test as well as a fact stated, that genuine knowledge of the Lord in resurrection life shows itself in an adoration of the Lord, worship of the Lord, devotion to the Lord Himself. If it is but the acceptance of a teaching it does not carry us that far. If it is the association with a movement we fall short of that. But if it is a personal knowledge of the Lord in the power of resurrection, the mark of our lives is a deep, reverent devotion to the Lord Himself. That is really the Testimony. It is not what we have to talk about. It is not our teaching, not our system of things, and not our movement. It is not even our fellowship as representing something

technical on the earth. It is our Lord! Let us never be found talk-
ing about the teaching which we have accepted, or which is represented by certain people in certain places. Let us see to it that
for us it is a matter of the Lord, and if the teaching does not
bring us to the Lord then there is something wrong, perhaps not
with the teaching, but with our apprehension of it. Worship must
become the dominating feature of those who know Him in the
power of His resurrection.

His Resources at the Lord's Disposal

The third thing noticeable is that Naaman wanted to place
his resources at the service of the Lord in offering a gift. That
has always been a feature of real life. It was so at Pentecost.
When the Lord does something within and brings into a new
fullness of Himself, we want all the fullness that we have to be
at the Lord's disposal. At any rate that was the inclination of the
heart of Naaman.

At this point we are brought to another consideration. There
was this proffered gift, but it was refused by Elisha simply
because a peril was recognized. Elisha had had no difficulty in
accepting material kindness at the hands of the Shunammite, but
he absolutely refused to accept anything at the hands of Naaman.
These two people stood in altogether different positions spiritually. The peril which Elisha clearly discerned in this particular
direction was lest Naaman should go away feeling that, after all,
he had some hand in this matter, and that he had paid for it. The
Lord never wants any gifts, any resources placed at His disposal
which carry with them the slightest suggestion that they are acts
of patronage. He leaves no room for any reactions of the flesh,
of nature, the gratifying of anything in that realm. So Elisha, recognizing that there might creep in, even at this point, some little
bit of that natural life which loves to have satisfaction in itself
because of what it does, closed the door to that, and refused to
admit any possibility of it. He sent Naaman away with the blessing, but with no personal gratification.

At that point the tragedy of Gehazi comes in. Gehazi saw what was done, and when Naaman had well begun his return journey, Gehazi went after him, made up a long story as from Elisha, his master, asked for the gift, and got it. We do not know what mischief that may have done with Naaman, but we do know that it brought Gehazi under a terrible judgment; "The leprosy before of Naaman shall cleave unto thee, and unto thy seed for ever."

What is the explanation of this? The Lord Jesus Himself seems to give us an insight into it in the Gospel by Luke, chapter iv. 27-29:

> And there were many lepers in Israel in the time of Elisha the prophet; and none of them was cleansed, but only Naaman the Syrian. And they were all filled with wrath in the synagogue, as they heard these things; And they rose up, and cast him forth out of the city. . . .

Gehazi had been in close touch with Elisha, had seen his works and heard his words, and all that Elisha represented was available to Gehazi; but Gehazi, with all his knowledge of it and association with it, remained upon a merely official ground, and never came on to a vital ground. Now we can see what the Lord is saying to the Jews. Without saying so in as many words, He has transferred the situation of Gehazi to the Jews of His own day: "You have heard: you have been in close association with the vessel of Life: you have seen the works: you know all about it from the standpoint of close proximity to it, *but* you remain merely upon official ground as ostensibly representing God, and have never come through on to living ground. Your judgment is leprosy, death!" That is what happened to Israel.

Gehazi stood on official ground. You see him acting in an official way when the Shunammite's son died, and she laid him on the bed of Elisha, and went to seek him. The prophet said to Gehazi, ". . . take my staff in thine hand, and go thy way . . . and lay my staff upon the face of the child." And we can see Gehazi taking the staff in his very official, pompous way, and going as the representative of the great prophet and putting the staff on the lad expecting to see some result, but nothing happened. Perhaps he tried moving the staff this way and that, to try to get some sort of response. But death never yields to what is merely official, death only yields to life. When the one who is in person the embodiment of life triumphant over death stretches himself upon that body, then death is swallowed up in life; but nothing official can do that.

The Jewish leaders were utterly impotent, although they were supposed to be the representatives of God. They were in close association with the life, yet they were dead. And because they did not come through to the position represented by Christ, but were self-seeking, like Gehazi (and their very self-seeking made them prejudiced) they came under judgment and perished. Their generations have been under that judgment ever since, and are there today. Leprosy and death clings to them for the age.

This is the warning side of things. It is possible to come into a very close proximity to the Testimony, to be in touch with things—to hear, to see, to know, to have an association which is formal—and yet never to stand livingly on that resurrection ground. It is a terrible tragedy to be in a position like that; and yet there are many, who can talk the dialect, use the phraseology, reproduce the terms, but who have not life. We may be in the privileges of association, and yet not in the life of union.

That word of warning cannot be left out as we come to the end of this story, but having struck the note of warning which we are obliged to admit into our consideration, let us close on the higher ground of noticing again to what the Lord calls us, and that is to an ever-growing knowledge of Himself in the power of His resurrection: and that increase of Divine life is by the way of a yielding up of our own interests, our own considerations. There is no life except by death. There is no gain except by loss.

May the Lord speak that message into our hearts according as it is necessary in our case.

CHAPTER SIX

The Throne in Heaven

2 Kings vi. 8-23.

When we reach this part of the life of Elisha, we come to touch an ultimate feature of the power of resurrection. It relates to the Throne in heaven. That which comes out of the sixth and seventh chapters of the second book of Kings is that secret, mystic touch which Elisha had with the Throne above. You are here getting away from the things which are more of an incidental character, back behind things, and you find that there is a secret, hidden communion between Elisha and the Throne of God in heaven. The very plans of the Syrian king, and his purposes, are divulged. Elisha has secret information apart from men, apart from all human observation. He knows within himself what is taking place. He is in touch with the Fountain Head of all knowledge, and it is by reason of the secret spiritual touch with the Throne that he so acts, and so moves, as to frustrate plans which would involve in death and destruction.

In New Testament words, Elisha comes to the place where he is not ignorant of the enemy's devices, but is cognizant of them. It is spiritual perception; it is spiritual knowledge. It is knowledge which springs from a spiritual union with the Throne of government in the heavens.

When the king of Syria seeks to take him, two other things of the same character come before us.

I. The Opening of the Eyes of Elisha's Servant

The Lord opened the eyes of Elisha's servant to see what his master was already seeing, that of which he was already aware, the spiritual hosts on the side of the Lord's servant.

Here again is union with the Throne in a very real way, and with all the Throne-resources.

II. Blindness Brought to the Syrian Host

In the same way by that union power is put forth to bring blindness upon the great host sent by the Syrian king to take him. Because of that touch with the Throne Elisha takes command of the opposing forces, and becomes the governor, the ruler, or one in command.

Here is a foreshadowing, in a sense, of what happened with Paul on his voyage to Rome. He began the voyage, humanly speaking, by being a prisoner, and concluded it by being both in command of the commander and of all under his command—the ship, the crew, and everything else. It was simply a case of spiritual ascendency because of his being in touch with the Throne.

Then again, the same thing is embodied in the turning of the famine recorded in chapter vii. There is a terrible and devastating famine, with horrible and ghastly aspects: the next day there is food obtainable for nearly nothing, and the hosts of the besieging army turning off because of a rumor, but so turned off as to leave all the provision of the hosts behind as resources for God's people. It is by the word of the Lord at the mouth of Elisha that this is done.

In all these matters you see two things, or two parts of one thing. There is the power of life triumphant over death, but this as representing a union with the Throne. And in recognizing that, we should recognize that the supreme, the ultimate issue and intention of knowing Him, and the power of His resurrection, even here in this life, is union with the Throne. It is heavenly union with the Lord.

This is where that foundational thing in the life of Elisha comes out in its fullest, its highest, and its deepest expression. That is to say, Elisha commenced his life ministry upon the establishment of a spiritual union with his master who had gone into heaven. The spirit of Elijah having fallen on Elisha made them one, and Elijah in heaven and Elisha on earth are in one-ness by reason of that spirit. All that comes through in the life of Elisha is simply the expression of what is implied by Elijah being in heaven.

In all this we can quite distinctly see the type of the exalta-tion of the Lord Jesus to the right hand of the Majesty on High. The Church as His instrument, His vessel on earth, is united with Him by the Holy Spirit, and is therefore in vital union with the Throne where He is. The Church is here to express the power, the dominion of that Throne of the ascended Lord. Into that all believers, individually and collectively, are called by the Lord.

Let us break that up, and first of all simply observe:

I. The Fact of Union With the Lord

It would not take us long in turning to the Word to establish the fact. We should only have to take one part of the Scriptures alone to establish that quite definitely, but there is a very great deal more. If we were to take the Gospel by John, we should find there that union with the Lord is one of the great features of that Gospel. It is illustrated in various ways right from the begin-ning—in the second chapter, the third chapter, the fourth chapter, the fifth chapter, the sixth chapter—right on it is one many-sided presentation of the truth of union with the Lord. And then there comes a point at which the Lord, having illustrated it, empha-sizes it. Having shown it to be the deepest reality of the relation-ship between Him and His disciples, and His disciples and Him-self, He begins to speak of going away, and says much about not tarrying, of there being but a little while and He will have gone. By such utterances He has provoked in them considerable con-cern, so that they are much troubled. Then, when that anxiety, that fear, that dread, that concern has reached a certain point of intensity in them, so that it is approaching the point of over-whelming depression, He changes the whole course of things with His word of exhortation, "Let not your heart be troubled. . . ." From that point He goes on to show that all that He has been saying about union is to be a spiritual thing of a deeper, stronger character than all His earthly association with them. He shows that although He is going, He is yet remaining; although He will be in heaven, He will still be in them. The union is a tremendous reality. He is saying quite clearly that this is far more real than the association of people on the earth.

You move from this Gospel to John's first epistle, and you know how much the same thing is emphasized there: ". . . our fellowship is with the Father, and with his Son. . . ." That is the basis of the epistle. The nature of that is expanded in the epistle, but we are not dealing with the nature, we are observing the fact of union with the Lord in heaven.

This is not merely the relationship between a god and his worshippers as in heathenism. There is a relationship between the gods of the heathen and their worshippers, but you can never call it a union. This is not relationship between a Creator and His creation. This is not a relationship as between a master and his servants, neither is this the relationship as of a workman and his tools. All these represent a relationship, but they never represent a union. What the Lord has designed is something very different from that kind of relationship. We fear that there are not a few people who know only that kind of relationship. God to them is a Creator, and they are His creation. God to them is God—perhaps the only true God—and they are worshippers of the true God. But that is not union. God has willed union. That is a great fact which is revealed throughout the Scriptures.

II. The Nature, Basis and Plan of This Union

(a) The Nature

The nature is that which carries it beyond such relationships as we have just mentioned. The nature of this relationship is essentially spiritual; that is, it is a union of spirit. "He that is joined to the Lord is one spirit." ". . . they that worship him must worship him in spirit . . ." because "God is a Spirit." The union, then, is the union of spirit. That goes deeper than any other kind of union. We cannot go deeper than that. That defines the nature of man in the deepest, the most real part of his being, that he is fundamentally in the sight of God, spirit.

(b) The Basis

The basis is life. That is what John brings out so clearly, by way of illustration, in his Gospel, and, by way of direct statement, in his epistle—". . . God gave unto us eternal life, and this life is in his Son." "He that hath the Son hath the life." That is a statement imposed upon the basic declaration that our fellowship is with the Father and with the Son. The fellowship is explained as being that of possessing His very life. The basis of union with God is that God's own life is given to us in new birth, and upon that God builds everything, on that He counts for everything. Where that is not, God can do nothing so far as union is concerned.

In order to reach and realize all God's thought, God must put Himself into man in the very essence of His being, His very life. God cannot realize spiritual, eternal, universal intentions on the basis of natural life. The Scriptures make it very clear that man's own natural life can never be the basis of the realization of any of God's purposes, that God's own life alone can be that. Thus for all His hopes God first of all provides His own basis. God's hope is in His own life, not in ours, and He puts the basis of His hope within at new birth, and on that basis He proceeds to the development of all His thought, and the realization of all His intention.

That life brings light. The light is the life. Without the life there can be no light. Light is essential, because man is not a will-less creature, but is destined to realize God's ends by cooperating intelligently with God on the basis of one life. Therefore, light is necessary; and if we walk in the light we have fellowship. The basis, then, of union is life, and life issues in light, by which again obedience comes.

You will notice that in all these activities of God in bringing about spiritual union with Himself, the Word is His instrument.

Life comes by the Word. Light comes by the Word. In the beginning of the creation, in bringing the creation into living union with Himself for His purposes, it was the Word first of all which was the instrument. In the re-creation, or regeneration, it is the Word again. "In the beginning was the Word," and it always is the Word. That is why the Lord Jesus said: ". . . the words that I speak unto you, they are spirit, and they are life." So that life and light by the Living Word are the basis of union with God.

(c) The Place

The place of union is "the inner man of the heart," to use the New Testament phrase. Paul was fond of using that phrase: ". . . our inward man is renewed day by day," ". . . that he would grant you . . . that ye may be strengthened with power through his Spirit in the inward man." What is the inward man? It is our spirit, the innermost place of our being. That is the seat of union. Union is not first of all physical in character. That needs no saying. Union between us and God is not in its genesis of a mental kind, neither is it of an emotional kind. Union between us and the Lord is not in the realm of our soul at all in the first instance. It is in our spirit. It is a thing which is deeper than our soul; that is, deeper than our reason, deeper than the powers of our natural mind either to analyze or understand. It is deeper than our emotions, deeper than our feelings. The fact of union with the Lord, when it is established, abides when all our feelings contradict it, and when all our power of reasoning is completely confounded. When in the realm of the reason and in the realm of the feelings there seems to be greatest evidence that the union does not exist, it remains. It is an important thing for the Lord's people to get that well settled, that union between us and the Lord has nothing whatever to do with our feelings nor our reasoning. If we sit down at times and allow our reasonings to carry us on, we shall conclude that the union does not exist, because there is so much which argues strongly and positively against any such union. If we allow our feelings, or our lack of feelings, to be the criterion, we shall give it all up and declare the whole thing to be a myth.

From time to time feelings are altogether against the fact of union with the Lord. It makes no difference; the union is there if it has been brought about. People who take the position that they must feel it or else they will not believe, are going to have a bad time. The same applies to people who demand that they shall be able to follow this thing through with the completest mental argument. The spiritual life is something which goes altogether beyond the range of man's mind. It is a very blessed thing to have that settled—provided there has really taken place that new birth, and there has been no positive, deliberate, conscious violation of the law of the new life, by which that life has been paralyzed, and shut up, and rendered for the time being inoperative because of disobedience; providing that we are going on in the light as we have it, and in obedience to the Lord. There will be times when the *sense* of the Lord will have disappeared from thee of our souls, and when everything in the realm of our minds seems to be confusion and contradiction. Nevertheless the fact abides, the union is there. He is more faithful than our feelings.

It is a great comfort to know that, when our feelings vary, and our sensations change, when perhaps by reason of physical and mental weariness those stronger spiritual sensations, as we would call them, disappear, and for a time we seem to drop down out of the realm of the higher ecstasies of the spiritual life, and things get flat. But after a little while it passes and we find the Lord is still there and we go on again. We come to understand that it was not the Lord who changed, but we were just having a bad time, and our bad time brought no basic change. We can cripple God by disobedience; we can paralyze Divine life by sinning against light; but even then ". . . if any man sin, we have an Advocate with the Father. . . ." John puts that in his letter in connection with fellowship, and it is a comfort. It simply says this: ". . . our fellowship is with the Father, and with his Son. . . ." We are to ". . . walk in the light, as he is in the light." As we do so ". . . the blood of Jesus Christ his Son cleanseth [Greek: keeps on cleansing] us from all sin."

The union is right deep down there in our spirit, deeper than the soul life in its variations, deeper than thought, deeper than feeling, yes, deeper than consciousness. In this matter our consciousness may not reach to the depths of God's work. You ask: "What do you mean by that?" We mean exactly what the book of Leviticus means, when we find there a distinct provision for someone who sins unconsciously. Is there such a thing as sinning unconsciously? That means that you have no consciousness about it, and yet it is sin. Consciousness is not the final rule. The final rule is God's standard, not our consciousness. Our consciousness, after all, is limited. God's standard is unlimited. God has provided in relation to His own standard, and not to the measure of our consciousness. That ought to help us. God has made provision right to the end of His demands, and not just to the measure of how much we are awake to those demands. God's work is deeper than anything that belongs to us.

III. The Issue of Union Is Government

All those features which we have mentioned are traceable in the sixth and seventh chapters of II Kings. Note the place of darkness—spiritual darkness as represented by the servant of Elisha, who could not see spiritual things. How does he come to apprehend spiritual things? Firstly, through his union with Elisha, who is the power of resurrection life, and then by reason of his union with him who is the life, he comes into the light. But what is the means? It is the Word. What is the result? Authority, ascendancy, dominion! It is coming at once from the place of fear and dread, as indicated in his words "Alas, my master! how shall we do?" to a place where he knows the truth—". . . they that be with us are more than they that be with them." We come into a place of great spiritual strength by enlightenment through union in life.

That opens a very wide sphere of important and very valuable contemplation. It would take us right out into the full range of God's intention. You notice it, by way of illustration, in the order of creation—first darkness, the Word of life, light, order, and then man placed in dominion. That is an illustration in creation of God's intention in the spiritual relationship between Himself and the new creation—chaos, darkness, the Word of life, light, fellowship, dominion. Follow that right through, and you will see that the purpose of God in Christ, as revealed in the New Testament, is to bring man to the Throne. That is illustrated in John's Gospel, or set forth in a spiritual way: ". . . where I am there, ye may be also." That as a spiritual fact is brought about at Pentecost by the Holy Spirit. You find that spiritually from that time onward the Lord's own were seen as in the place of absolute spiritual ascendancy and dominion. You see it very fully represented in the life of the Apostle Paul himself right to the end. Whatever may be the circumstances, the conditions of his life down here on earth, he is spiritually in union with the Throne above, so that even in a prison he never calls himself Caesar's prisoner, never refers to himself as the prisoner of Nero. He calls himself the prisoner of Jesus Christ, and in his prison, despite the earthly limitations, he is moving about in the limitless expanses of the heavenly places: he is no prisoner. He knows spiritually the meaning of union with his Lord above, and that is the secret of his fruitfulness and effectiveness of life.

Definite statements are made from time to time as to this thought of God. "To him that overcometh will I grant to sit with me in my throne, even as I also overcame, and am set down with my Father in his throne." God's thought is that. Now it is spiritual; then it will be literal. Now it is inward union with Him in His Throne, with spiritual power and ascendancy over all other forces; then it will be manifested in its full, literal way—universal dominion through the Church.

This is the very nature of resurrection life. It is all bound up with our apprehension of the death, resurrection and exaltation of Christ. How do you apprehend the death of Christ? Do you apprehend the death of Christ as the death and putting away of a man who could never reign, who could never come to the

Throne? Adam, after sin, could never come to the Throne; God could not put a man like that in dominion. Adam lost his dominion. God will never bring fallen man to dominion. The death of Christ puts away judicially the man who could never reign, to make room for a Man Who can reign. The resurrection of the Lord Jesus brings in the Man Who can reign. Do we apprehend the resurrection of the Lord Jesus as the bringing into being of another Man Who can go on to the Throne? The very essence of our resurrection-union with the Lord Jesus is the union of one life between Him as there in the Throne and ourselves as here. How do you apprehend the exaltation of the Lord Jesus? Do you apprehend it as your exaltation representatively? Do you apprehend that when He died, you died, when He rose, you rose? It is a spiritual reality. Now that which was born of the flesh has gone; in resurrection it is that which is born of the Spirit, the spiritual man. That is you in resurrection with the Lord Jesus! And what is true of the death and resurrection, is true of the exaltation, that when He was exalted *you were exalted* in Him at the right hand of the Majesty on High. Have we grasped that Christ's being there is our being there in representation? That is not just some objective truth, but is made real by reason of His ascended life being now within us, and the Holy Spirit having created the living link between Him in heaven and ourselves as here. The fact that He is above all says that we in Him are also above all.

You say: "That may be true theoretically, doctrinally true, and I do not dispute what is said, but that is not true in my case." That is not the Lord's fault! It is because we have not learned to live on the basis of His resurrection life. We have still tried to live a Christian life on the basis of our own life, and that can never come to the Throne. People who are trying to be Christians by effort, by endeavor of their own, are always far from reaching the Throne. They are the playthings of all the forces which are antagonistic to Christ. But when we know the secret of living on His life by the Holy Spirit, we know in a growing, a progressive way, that it is true that He is not there apart from us, but that there is a union between Him in dominion and ourselves in the power of His Own life. Resurrection life is in itself the very life of Christ in dominion. Whenever resurrection life in us has its way, it brings us into dominion. Whenever there is a working of His life freely in us, it puts us in a place of ascendancy, it lifts us above, it is spiritual power and dominion.

IV. The Law of Union Is Faith

Here faith in the Lord Jesus becomes something more than perhaps we have hitherto realized. What is faith in Christ? It is the recognition of what He is at God's right hand for us and as us. There is a Humanity, a Man who has passed right through and realized in every detail all God's thought for us, and God's thought for us is reached, fully and finally, in a Man. That Man has everything (not for Himself but for us) that is necessary to bring us to God's end. Christ is our Victory; Christ is our Life; Christ is our Wisdom; Christ is our Sanctification. There is nothing in all the catalogue of needs, in order to bring us to God's full thought, but what Christ is made *that* unto us, and faith makes that living by taking it and acting upon it.

Is the enemy raging? Christ has conquered, and is the Victor over the enemy. Faith brings Him in, and puts Christ over against the situation in which the enemy is so active. Whatever it may be that threatens to limit our coming to God's thought, Christ is the provision to meet that. But He only does so along the line of our faith. Faith in Christ is a wonderful thing. What you and I have to learn more and more is to bring Christ into the situation on our behalf, whatever the need may be, so that we live by Christ. There will always be a whole list of "I cannots," so far as we are concerned, but are we going to stop with "I cannot"? Or are we going to recognize once and for all that we cannot? That is settled! We need not say any more! But that is just where His "can" begins, and we do not stop short at a negative, we start at the positive—"I can do all things through Christ. . . ."

It is a challenge to us as to faith in Christ. It is bringing Christ into every situation. That is government, dominion. That is the Throne, because He is the exalted, reigning Christ.

We are glad that He is there in that position: "And he put all things in subjection under his feet, and gave him to be head over all things to the church, which is his body, the fullness of him that filleth all in all." Faith recognizes that; faith sees that; faith applies that. It is what Christ is in heaven.

The course of things is that at the beginning we have union *in* Christ with the Father; at the end we have union *with* Christ *in* the Father. That is what the Word teaches. Firstly, our union is in Christ with the Father; then the Word shows that the end of the process is eventually union with Christ in the Father.

Union is a progressive thing. Faith at present operates in the direction of our union in Christ with the Father. Faith works out eventually to bring us in union with Christ in the Father. This does not mean—is it necessary to say?—absorption in the God-head, or participation in Deity.

The main point of our consideration is that resurrection life, the power of His resurrection, is essentially in its nature a Throne union with the Lord, and that that is to have a practical outworking in a spiritual way now. Ultimately it will have a literal outworking universally. Our business at present is to learn how to reign in life by the One Man, Jesus Christ. The Lord teach us what it means to reign in life.

CHAPTER SEVEN

Closing Scenes

2 Kings xiii. 14-25.

In these verses we read of the closing scenes in the life of
Elisha. There are three things which stand out.

    I. The arrow of the Lord's deliverance.
    II. The smiting of the ground with the arrows.
    III. The body of the dead soldier reviving by contact with
        Elisha's body.

These three instances are a very fitting conclusion to the life
of Elisha in the light of the spiritual meaning of his life, namely,
that he represents throughout the power of resurrection life; that
is, testimony in life all the way through, is one of testimony
against death in various and numerous forms. Here we have
Elisha at the end, but how wonderfully the life is maintained.

How suited to all that has gone before are these incidents.
Life triumphant over death right through to the last! Although it
says that he was sick of his sickness whereof he died, that is only
one aspect. That relates to the human vessel. There is another
side where Elisha never did die. When the human vessel has
gone, even then the testimony to life triumphant over death is
maintained, so that the very dead are quickened by that testimony, which goes on when the vessel has departed. It is mighty
life.

Here is Elisha on his bed, an old man, on the human side in
weakness, and so soon to pass away. The king of Israel comes to
him, and he lifts himself in his bed, calls to the king to bring his
bow and his arrows, and to put the arrow in the bow. Then the
prophet places his hands over the hands of the king, they two

draw the bow to its full extent, and that arrow goes in the power of resurrection life from that bed through the open window. The life of resurrection is in that arrow. Life triumphant over death is the strength of that arrow of the Lord's deliverance.

Then there comes the command to the king to smite the ground with his arrows, and he smites thrice and stays. The man of God is wroth with him There is still much more energy in the dying prophet than there is in the living king. He is the very embodiment of energy to the end. In effect he says: "Why did you not go on; why did you stop so soon; why did you not go right through with the whole thing?" He breathes life and energy.

Then, even when his body is dead and in the tomb, contact with it is life. It is a marvelous conclusion, full of significance and spiritual value. Nothing could more aptly fit into his whole testimony. You could have no finer conclusion and rounding off than that. It would have been a disappointing thing had Elisha just gone as if something of a tragedy had overtaken him and he had fallen a prey to some evil and been killed, or had he simply disappeared from the scene. You can never associate such a thing with that which all the way through represents triumph over death in every direction. You expect that testimony to be maintained right through and beyond, going out of time into eternity. And so it is. That life triumphant over death is something which does not end here, it goes on. It is a testimony which outlives its vessels.

Turning to the three instances we shall seek to understand in some measure what they have to say to us specifically. There are depths and fullnesses in all these incidents in Elisha's life, and in his life as a whole, which we cannot stay to touch upon. But there are some things which seem more or less apparent as lessons to be learned by us in these three closing incidents of Elisha's life.

I. The Arrow of the Lord's Deliverance

It was a question of victory over the enemy. And it is a matter of the Lord's purpose to give full and final victory over the enemy. What the king of Israel entered into may be one thing, what the Lord's thought was is another. He may only have come into it in a limited way, but that was his own fault. The Lord provided for very much more than that. We shall come back to that in a moment.

The thing from the Divine standpoint is the overcoming, fully and finally, of the Lord's enemy. The fullness of deliverance and victory was bound up in Elisha's prophecy. Although for the time being, because of the limited appropriation of the king, the representative of the Lord's people, that prophecy will be long postponed in its full realization, nevertheless the arrow of the Lord's deliverance has been released, and, in spite of postponement, ultimately the Lord's people will have a complete and full deliverance. It is secured to them in the prophecy. This arrow of deliverance is the arrow of a prophecy, the fuller expression of which may be found in the other prophets, such as Ezekiel and his vision of the valley of dry bones, the triumphant side of the activity of the resurrection of the Lord's people, and their ultimate standing upon their feet a mighty army. It is all bound up in this arrow of deliverance. But more than that, there is foreseen in the illustration, in the type, the ultimate full triumph of the people of God spiritually over the last enemy. "The last enemy that shall be destroyed is death." The guarantee, the earnest, the title deeds of the final triumph over the last enemy, death, is in the fact that resurrection life is already given to the Lord's people.

The last enemy will be overcome in the Church, the Body of Christ, by the power of His resurrection. The Church has been long entering into the value of that. The Church has known, because of its own weakness, only a little of that, but eventually it will be realized to the full. The Word of the Lord is full of that fact, that the end is going to see the last enemy destroyed in the Church. It is to be in the Church, the Body of Christ, that the last enemy is destroyed, and that death is to be finally cast out.

The earnest of that is the fact that Christ, already triumphant over death, is resident within His Body. Take such passages as

Ephesians i. 17-21. There is seen universal dominion resultant from the inworking of the power of His resurrection. To put that round the other way in the terms of this Scripture, "the exceeding greatness of his power"—which is that of resurrection—by which God raised Jesus from the dead issues in universal authority. Thus universal authority over all the power of the enemy is resident within the power of His resurrection. Resurrection life contains that very power by which death shall be fully and finally vanquished, and the Church, the Body of Christ, knowing that power (". . . that the God of our Lord Jesus Christ . . . may give unto you a spirit of wisdom and revelation in the knowledge of him . . . that ye may *know* . . . the exceeding greatness of his power . . .") will come to the place where the Head already is.

Pass from that passage to the third chapter of the same letter, verse 20, and you have similar things said: ". . . according to the power that worketh in us." What power is that? "The exceeding greatness of his power . . . which he wrought in Christ, when he raised him from the dead. . . ." "Unto him be the glory *in the church* and in Christ Jesus unto all generations for ever and ever." Here is resurrection.

Let us repeat, that the last enemy, death, is going to be finally and fully overthrown in and by the Church, on the basis of the resurrection life of the Lord Jesus operating in that Church as the Body of Christ. Herein is the necessity for you and for me *now* to learn to live on the basis of resurrection life. Herein is the explanation of why the Lord takes pains to bring us to the place where only His risen life will meet our need. Herein is the explanation of the constant application of the Cross to cut from under us every other basis of life save the life of the Lord, because of the enormous issue involved, that the Church is the chosen means by which the risen Head is to settle finally the issue of death.

That brings us to an interesting and significant point in this story of Elisha. Do you notice how the king of Israel addresses Elisha? Look at verse 14 of chapter xiii, and you will see there an extraordinary address. What did he mean? Was he expecting Elisha to go the same way as Elijah? Was it an expression of some feeling that Elisha was about to be raptured? I confess I do not know from the standpoint of Joash. But I think I can stand on the side of the Holy Spirit and see some meaning, because if the Holy Spirit inspired this, then there is a spiritual meaning. Elijah went up into heaven in a chariot of fire amidst the shouts of Elisha—"My father, my father, the chariot of Israel and the horsemen thereof!" That was Elijah's victory over death. We do not have that form of victory with Elisha, but we have the same words. Elisha did not go into heaven by a chariot of fire, as did Elijah, nevertheless exactly the same words apply to him. He comes within exactly the same category of those who conquer death and are not conquered by death. But what is the difference? If Elijah was raptured outwardly, Elisha was raptured inwardly, but it is the same thing. Resurrection life in any case is rapture in its issue. It is victory in its outworking. It is victory over death, and victory over death is rapture. What is rapture ? It is glory! And, so far as the principle and basis of rapture is concerned, which is the power of His resurrection, that holds good whatever may be the form of its outward consummation.

Was not Paul as truly at the end of his life, as he had hoped to be at the beginning? When you read his first letters, the letters to the Thessalonians, there is no doubt but that Paul thought and hoped to be raptured with the Church—". . . *we* which are alive and remain shall be caught up. . . ." After many years, toward the end, he came to see that that was not to be the manner of his going, and said so quite frankly. ". . . I am already being offered, and the time of my departure is come." And he knew by what method it would be. But spiritually in his inner life he was as truly raptured at the end as he had hoped to be at the beginning. It was not death, it was not defeat, it was not the mastery of death; it was victory over death, triumph over death. It was glory. He could go through in perfect confidence and perfect triumph; he could go through with a shout in his spirit. Though the executioner's axe is about to be lifted to sever his head from his body, he could go through with a shout—"the chariot of Israel and the horsemen thereof"! He is above the whole thing. Whatever may be the course, resurrection life embodies rapture in itself. So that, whether Elijah goes up literally in a chariot, or Elisha goes up spiritually in a chariot, it is the same in the working out.

But there is something more. Paul had two phases of resurrection in his heart and in his faith. Firstly he had resurrection inwardly. The power of resurrection was at work in him all the time, so that death was being transcended in all its workings. In his spirit he was always above death. He knew the power of resurrection as an inward thing.

But then, in the second place, Paul had his heart and his faith set upon a specific form of its outworking, in what he called uniquely "the out-resurrection from among the dead." It is Paul who brings into view such a thing. His desire and ambition was not just to attain unto the resurrection from the dead. You have to do nothing to attain unto the resurrection from the dead. If you are saved you will enjoy the resurrection from the dead without any attaining whatever. The fact that you have eternal life is the guarantee that you will be raised from the dead. The Lord Jesus made that perfectly clear, that He would give unto as many as He would eternal life and raise them up at the last day. But there is a day which anticipates the last day, and that was the day that Paul was after. He did not speak of the last day resurrection, he spoke of the out-resurrection from among the dead. This for him represented rapture, in which not even all those who are the Lord's will participate. If Philippians iii. 10 means anything at all, if language is to be taken seriously, it does most definitely indicate that this resurrection is not that general resurrection which comes with the gift of eternal life, but this is a prize. Resurrection from the dead in general is not a prize. It accompanies the free gift of God. A prize is always something worked for, striven after, and which may be missed, as Paul makes perfectly clear. This out-resurrection is a prize which extends him fully.

That is where the first phase of this chapter ends and makes necessary the second phase, because the one arrow must lead to the other arrows.

II. The Smiting on the Ground With the Arrows

Elisha does not leave things with the releasing of that one arrow, prophetic of full and final deliverance, but he instantly takes another course, by which he would seek to bring the king at once into the full possession of it, to anticipate the end, and to secure it in advance. It might have been that Elisha had said when the one arrow was released: "The arrow of the Lord's deliverance! Someday—it may be a long way ahead—there will be full deliverance. This arrow declares it." He might just have left it there, and that would have meant a measure of comfort, the comfort which you get from 1 Thess. iv. 16, that ultimately all the saints will be raised, those who have gone and those that remain. The thing will come into the final victory at some time. That is a general statement. What we read in Thessalonians is but a general statement, and you need a great deal more Scripture to get inside of the general statement. Paul there is only making quite a comprehensive statement, he is not giving us anything more. We need much more to break that up. It is not fair to take the general statement, and say that is the beginning and the end of all the doctrine of the rapture, or the resurrection, or the coming of the Lord. It is not by any means!

Elisha does not leave things there. He says to Joash: "Take the arrows. . . . Smite upon the ground." Anticipate the end, get hold of it now, make it good now. And Joash takes his arrows and smites once, twice, thrice, and stays. And Elisha asks why he has stayed, why he accepts less than he might have, why he does not go the full way now and possess the whole at once— ". . . now thou shalt smite Syria but thrice." That will be your measure of glory. Whereas you might have gone right on and had so much more glory, known so much more ascendancy and victory, you have fixed the measure yourself.

See how wonderfully that fits into Phil. iii. The measure of victory and glory will be the measure of faith's appropriation of the power of His resurrection. We are not dealing with the matter of salvation now, we are dealing with God's full thought as to salvation. And when Paul wrote that letter to the Philippians and came to the part of his letter which is marked by our third chapter, it was as though he smote, and he smote, and he smote, until he had the whole thing—". . . but one thing I do, forgetting the things which are behind . . ." (it was the uttermost taking hold of Him and the power of His resurrection) ". . . that I may know him . . . if by any means I may attain unto the out-resurrection [Greek]. . . ." There is a man who does not stay short of the whole end of God.

The Lord's people are going to come more or less to the fullness of the glory of Christ, more or less to the place of universal dominion, according to the measure of faith's appropriation now of the power of His resurrection. Paul says in another place that in the resurrection there are differences of degree, that there is one glory of the sun, and another glory of the moon, and another glory of the stars, and that so shall it be in the resurrection. Do you want the glory of the sun, the full-orbed glory of Christ? Well, that demands now a going the whole way in the matter of faith's appropriation of the power of His resurrection—". . . that life which I now live in the flesh I live in faith, the faith which is in the Son of God," and then, with that basis laid, a pressing on to know Him, and the power of His resurrection.

The point is that there is something to be lost. That may not be our salvation, but that may be glory in measure, positions which the Lord would have us occupy and enjoy, but from which we may fall short. The Word of God points out that the generation of Hebrews which fell in the wilderness lost their inheritance. And Paul carries that principle forward when he says that you can be saved, but only as by fire. You may not lose your salvation, but you may lose everything else that God intended you to have in your salvation. There is something which God has which we can only have on conditions. And when we view that in the light of God's own need, "his inheritance in the saints," and of God's own purpose, and when we view it in the light of what it has cost God and His Son, it becomes a sin to be satisfied with less than all that God desires. The Lord Jesus did not suffer all that Calvary meant just to get us out of hell, just to get us saved. There is far more than that bound up in His Cross. This has a good deal of light to throw upon the New Testament position.

III. The Revival of a Dead Body by Contact With Elisha's Bones

"Now the bands of the Moabites invaded the land at the coming in of the year. And as they were burying a man . . . they spied a band; and they cast the man into the sepulchre of Elisha; and as soon as the man touched the bones of Elisha, he revived, and stood up on his feet."

The knowing of Christ in the power of His resurrection is by conformity to His death. It is on the ground of identification with Him in death. Here is this man falling into the sepulchre of Elisha and becoming identified with him in his death. Typically he came to the place mentioned by Paul ". . . that I may know him, and the power of his resurrection, and the fellowship of his sufferings, *being made conformable unto his death.*" But that very conformity to His death was the way of knowing the power of His resurrection. That very identification with Him in death issued in resurrection life.

We must always remember that the death of the Lord Jesus is not a passive thing. The death of the Lord Jesus is a mighty energy, a mighty power. There is something about the death of the Lord Jesus which death cannot stand. His very death swallowed up death; His very death destroyed death—". . . that through death he might destroy him that had the power of death." There is a mystery about that, how a death can kill death, but it did in His case. The death of the Lord Jesus is not the death of any other man: it is a different death, a mighty death, an energetic death.

This man touched the bones of Elisha and found that in the place of death there was victory over death, power destroying death.

That ought to be a very strong additional word to our ideas about identification with Christ in death, because so often people think that when language like that is used it means going out and losing everything; it is all death, death, death! You never do touch the Lord Jesus in His death in any new measure without knowing a new measure of resurrection life. When the Lord Jesus by His Spirit brings us in a further measure into the meaning of His death, let it be settled with us, once and for all, that that is in itself a new measure of resurrection life. The two things go together, it cannot be otherwise. It is death unto life. It is loss unto gain. The life and the gain are of a different sort from the death and the loss. The death and the loss is simply all that which, sooner or later, will go in any case, and even while it remains is of a very doubtful value, but the life and the gain are eternal, and have in them all the values of God. So Paul could, with something of joy, hail conformity to the death of Christ. He speaks about it in no mournful terms as though he were going to lose everything. There is no shadow on his face or sob in his voice when he speaks about being conformed to His death. It is the shout of a victor. There is something he is after.

Paul knows quite well the value of this exchange, the exchanging of his life for the life of His Lord, the exchange of which he has been speaking in this very letter—"Howbeit what things were gain to me, these have I counted loss for Christ . . . for the excellency of the knowledge of Christ Jesus my Lord." What is the nature of that knowledge? "That I may know him, and the power of his resurrection." That is the excelling quality of this knowledge. It excels everything that could come to a man in this world, that would be regarded by a man of this world as gain, and he has tabulated and catalogued all those things. He has known power, popularity, reputation, position, possession, and he says the knowledge of Christ Jesus is excelling all that. What knowledge is it? It is the particular knowledge of "him, and the power of his resurrection." Why? Because of what that leads to, all the possibilities of that resurrection life and power: because of its ultimate issue: because of the place to which it can bring him; no less a place than the very Throne of the Lord Himself.

We have left out a good many things, and have not pursued the various lines and questions that may have arisen, content just to give the broad outline of the many features. Questions may have arisen, but let us first of all face the facts and say: Are these facts? Get rid of prejudices, and ask broad questions—"Why should I not accept that? What is there to hinder?" If we are very frank and open, without prejudice in matters like this, we shall get light, and that light will mean a very great deal. But if we have preconceived ideas, preconceptions strongly held, we shall get into a fog as we touch these matters. An open heart provides the way for the Lord to give much light. A willingness to accept what is of the Lord makes it possible for the Lord to show what is of Himself.

Leaving for the moment all the details, let us look at the statements squarely in the face, confront ourselves with the mighty "ifs." *"If* by *any means* I may attain unto the out-resurrection [Greek]. . . ." What hangs upon an "if"! We may take it that it is not our salvation that hangs upon an "if." Our salvation hangs upon Christ's finished work and our faith therein. But there is something which hangs upon an "if." The Lord inspire us with His own mighty urge, and the inward working of His exceeding great power unto the full end, that we shall not fall short of His thought.

SeedSowers
P.O. Box 3317
Jacksonville, FL 32206
800-228-2665

904-598-3456 (fax)   www.seedsowers.com

REVOLUTIONARY BOOKS ON CHURCH LIFE

The House Church Movement (*Begier, Richey, Vasiliades, Viola*) 9.9
How to Meet In Homes (*Edwards*) 10.9
An Open Letter to House Church Leaders (*Edwards*) 4.0
When the Church Was Led Only by Laymen (Edwards) 4.0
Beyond Radical (*Edwards*) 5.9
Rethinking Elders (*Edwards*) 9.9
Revolution, The Story of the Early Church (*Edwards*) 8.9
The Silas Diary (*Edwards*) 9.9
The Titas Diary (*Edwards*) 8.9
The Timothy Diary (*Edwards*) 9.9
The Priscilla Diary (*Edwards*) 9.9
Overlooked Christianity (*Edwards*) 14.9

AN INTRODUCTION TO THE DEEPER CHRISTIAN LIFE

Living by the Highest Life (*Edwards*) 8.9
The Secret to the Christian Life (*Edwards*) 8.9
The Inward Journey (*Edwards*) 8.9

CLASSICS ON THE DEEPER CHRISTIAN LIFE

Experiencing the Depths of Jesus Christ (*Guyon*) 8.9
Practicing His Presence (*Lawrence/Laubach*) 8.9
The Spiritual Guide (*Molinos*) 8.9
Song of the Bride (*Guyon*) 9.9
Union With God (*Guyon*) 8.9
The Seeking Heart (*Fenelon*) 9.9
Intimacy with Christ (*Guyon*) 14.9
Spiritual Torrents (*Guyon*) 14.9
The Ultimate Intention (*Fromke*) 11.0

IN A CLASS BY THEMSELVES

The Divine Romance (*Edwards*) 8.9
The Story of My Life as told by Jesus Christ (Four gospels blended) 14.9
Acts in First Person 9.9

THE CHRONICLES OF THE DOOR *(Edwards)*

The Beginning 8.99
The Escape 8.99
The Birth 8.99
The Triumph 8.99
The Return 8.99

THE WORKS OF T. AUSTIN-SPARKS

The Centrality of Jesus Christ 19.95
The House of God 29.95
Ministry 29.95
Service 19.95

COMFORT AND HEALING

A Tale of Three Kings *(Edwards)* 8.99
The Prisoner in the Third Cell *(Edwards)* 5.99
Letters to a Devastated Christian *(Edwards)* 5.95
Healing for those who have been Crucified by Christians *(Edwards)* 8.95
Dear Lillian *(Edwards)* 5.95

OTHER BOOKS ON CHURCH LIFE

Climb the Highest Mountain *(Edwards)* 9.95
The Torch of the Testimony *(Kennedy)* 14.95
The Passing of the Torch *(Chen)* 9.95
Going to Church in the First Century *(Banks)* 5.95
When the Church was Young *(Loosley)* 14.95
Church Unity *(Litzman, Nee, Edwards)* 14.95
Let's Return to Christian Unity *(Kurosaki)* 14.95

CHRISTIAN LIVING

Final Steps in Christian Maturity *(Guyon)* 12.95
Turkeys and Eagles *(Lord)* 8.95
Beholding and Becoming *(Coulter)* 8.95
Life's Ultimate Privilege *(Fromke)* 7.00
Unto Full Stature *(Fromke)* 7.00
All and Only *(Kilpatrick)* 7.95
Adoration *(Kilpatrick)* 8.95
Release of the Spirit *(Nee)* 5.00
Bone of His Bone *(Huegel)* 8.95
Christ as All in All *(Haller)* 9.95

* call for a free catalog 800-228-2665